100
CREATIVE WAYS
~ To Use ~
ROTISSERIE CHICKEN
in Everyday Meals

TRISH ROSENQUIST
FOUNDER OF MOM ON TIMEOUT

PAGE STREET
PUBLISHING CO.

PAGE STREET
PUBLISHING CO.

First published in 2015 by
Page Street Publishing Co.
27 Congress Street, Suite 103
Salem, MA 01970
www.pagestreetpublishing.com

Distributed by Macmillan, sales in Canada by The Canadian Manda Group.

18 17 16 15   1 2 3 4 5

ISBN-13: 9781624141782
ISBN-10: 1624141781

Library of Congress Control Number: 2015938777

Cover and book design by Page Street Publishing Co.
Photography by Trish Rosenquist

Printed and bound in China

Page Street is proud to be a member of 1% for the Planet. Members donate one percent of their sales to one or more of the over 1,500 environmental and sustainability charities across the globe who participate in this program.

TO MY MOM, WHO INSPIRES ME EVERY SINGLE DAY. THANK YOU FOR ALWAYS BELIEVING IN ME AND ENCOURAGING ME TO DO MY BEST. I MISS YOU.

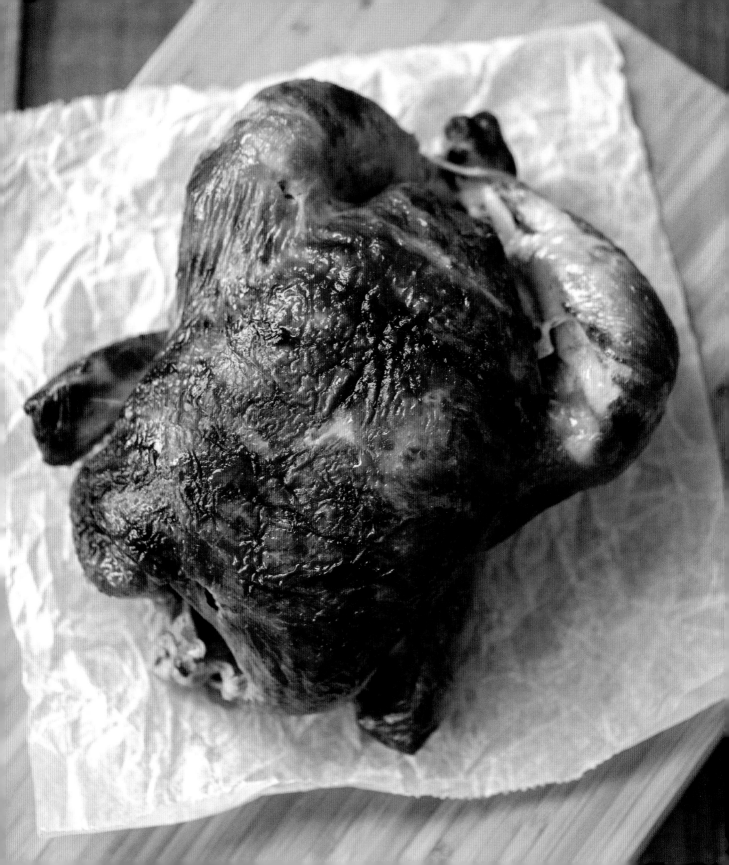

INTRODUCTION

Welcome! I am so excited that you've decided to save some time in the kitchen with these easy dinner recipes that use rotisserie chicken. For me, life happens in the kitchen, and more importantly, around the dinner table. As much as I love cooking and baking meals for my family, I love spending time with them even more.

Saving time, while still creating delicious and interesting meals for my family, is the true inspiration behind this book. There isn't much that I love more than a good shortcut in the kitchen, and rotisserie chicken is one of my favorites. I have been enjoying cooking with and eating rotisserie chicken for years and have come to rely on it when creating meals for my family. Straight from the store you've got perfectly cooked chicken that is moist, tender and flavorful—perfection!

I love how easy it is to incorporate rotisserie chicken into family favorites. While rotisserie chicken is delicious on its own, it is an equally amazing and versatile ingredient for many recipes. I remember the incredible response I received when I shared my first rotisserie chicken recipe on my blog, *Mom On Timeout*—it was overwhelmingly positive. I realized right then and there that many families are in the same position that I am in: They want to prepare delicious and creative meals and are happy to use a healthy shortcut when possible.

As a mom, I want my boys to be exposed to a wide variety of food. We love to try new recipes out and find new favorites to add to the menu. I'm not a big fan of "sneaking" vegetables, into dinner to get my kids to eat them. I want them to know that the meal has vegetables, and then, when they like what they're eating, they can see that *hey, veggies aren't that bad*.

You'll notice that most of the recipes have vegetables in them—some more than others. I wish I could say it's because I'm a SUPER HEALTHY mom, but the truth is that it's because I'm lazy. Incorporating veggies into each recipe ensures that my boys actually EAT them, and that's just how I roll.

GETTING TO KNOW YOUR ROTISSERIE CHICKEN

When I first started incorporating rotisserie chicken in recipes, I'm afraid to say I wasn't doing a terrific job at breaking it down. If you haven't spent a lot of time breaking down a chicken, I suggest you do that the next time you pick up a rotisserie chicken for some extra practice. There are a lot of hidden pockets of tender, juicy meat that really shouldn't be wasted.

The majority of the meat on the chicken is in the breasts. The legs and thighs are second, and the wings are last. I usually hand a wing to each of my boys to eat instead of trying to pick the meat off, since it's so bony.

Most of the recipes in this book don't require the skin of the chicken, so if you know that the recipe you are planning on making requires just the meat, go ahead and remove the skin.

DO I HAVE TO USE ROTISSERIE CHICKEN IN THESE RECIPES?

The short answer to that question is no. The purpose of this book is to provide you with a myriad of recipes that are easy to make, convenient and, of course, delicious. The key component of this book is *convenience*. If you have leftover cooked chicken—whether it's roasted, grilled or fried—it most likely can be used for a number of recipes in this book.

It's important to use your best judgment in determining if a substitution will taste good.

For example, a lemon-tarragon roasted chicken might not work so well for the Chicken Nachos Supreme (page 41), but leftover grilled chicken would be ideal for the BBQ Chicken Loaded Baked Potatoes (page 35) or the Monterey Chicken Pinwheels (page 66).

While these recipes were written to be made with rotisserie chicken, substitutions can always be made.

SAVE THOSE DRIPPINGS

What's that stuff you see on the bottom of the rotisserie chicken container? It's the drippings! Trust me when I say that this stuff is like liquid gold. I pour all of the drippings in a jar and save them with every rotisserie chicken that I buy. If you chill the chicken before pulling the meat, you will notice that the drippings have turned into a gel-like substance. Just scrape it off of the chicken and its container, place it in an airtight container and refrigerate for later use. The drippings can be used to make gravy or added to any soup recipe that calls for chicken broth—it will add so much depth and flavor to the dish!

NOT ALL ROTISSERIE CHICKENS ARE CREATED EQUAL

I have bought hundreds of rotisserie chickens over the last 10 years, and I can tell you for a fact that not all are created equal. First of all, let's talk about size. I have seen rotisserie chickens that range from 1 ½ pounds (680 g) up to 4 pounds (1.8 kg). When buying a rotisserie chicken, consider the cost, weight and freshness of the chicken. You want the best combination of all three to ensure a good product.

WHERE TO BUY

I buy most of my rotisserie chickens from Costco. The price is reasonable, the chicken is cooked perfectly every time and it's readily available. Not everyone does or can shop at Costco, so keep these points in mind when purchasing your rotisserie chicken:

* Shop at a store with high turnover—you want to buy the freshest chicken possible.

* Know your store—most local grocery stores keep to a schedule for their rotisserie chickens (e.g., 11am, 4pm, 6pm). Make sure you know yours!

* Consistent quality—using good-quality chicken is important to yield the tastiest dishes. Most stores label their chicken free-range, antibiotic free, etc.

STORING YOUR ROTISSERIE CHICKEN

After buying your rotisserie chicken, you should let it rest for a while before pulling the meat off the bones. I live about 20 minutes away from the store where I purchase my rotisserie chickens, so by the time I get home and put the rest of the groceries away, the chickens are usually cool enough to handle. If the chicken is too hot to handle, it's not ready to have the meat pulled off just yet.

You can always refrigerate the chicken immediately, but I have found that it's harder to pull the thigh and leg meat off the bone when it is cold.

I like to leave the chicken in pieces that are as large as possible because I may not necessarily know how I'm going to use it. For instance, if I end up making sandwiches, I want to be able to slice the chicken breast into nice thick slices, but if it's pulled to bits, it becomes harder to do so. Leaving the breasts intact will give you more options later on.

Once the meat has been removed from the bones, it's time to package and store your chicken in the refrigerator. I do this in one of two ways. The first is to put it in a resealable bag, making sure you compress all of the air out of the bag before zipping it closed. The second way is to put it in an airtight container. When using the latter method, I frequently separate the dark and white meats into different containers so that I can easily pull out the type of meat needed for a recipe.

Writing this book has been a process, to say the least. It was so much more work than I anticipated but equally more rewarding. I hope you and your family will find many new family favorites inside. Let's get cooking!

CHAPTER 1

CASSEROLES, BAKES AND MORE

Casseroles. Is there anything better? They are the quintessential comfort food and encompass all of the qualities that busy moms, such as myself, look for in a recipe: easy to prepare, kid-approved and delicious!

Whether I'm serving up favorites such as my Loaded Baked Potato Casserole (page 14) or Crunchy Potato Chip Casserole (page 25) or introducing new dishes like the Cornbread Taco Bake (page 22), I know my family will eat every last bite!

If you're a novice in the kitchen, casseroles are a great place to start. They're inherently forgiving and incredibly adaptable to best suit your family's preferences.

Make sure to check out my three favorites: the crowd-pleasing Cheesy Chicken, Broccoli and Rice Casserole (page 17), Chicken Cordon Bleu Pasta Casserole (page 18) and Chicken Pot Pie (page 20)!

ROTISSERIE CHICKEN CASSEROLE

YIELD: 6 SERVINGS

This is the rotisserie chicken recipe that started it all. I have been making this casserole for more than two decades. I first started making it when I was about 10 years old, and it's since remained one of my very favorite recipes. I used to boil the chicken, but then I got married. And had kids. And got tired. I turned to rotisserie chicken as a shortcut, and that's when my love for this convenient food began.

Rice and chicken are made for each other, and that's especially true when they're paired in a comforting casserole. We enthusiastically devour this casserole for dinner, but I have also been known to sneak leftovers for breakfast—*hey! there are corn flakes on the top!*

2 cups (250 g) diced rotisserie chicken

1 (10 ¾ oz [305 ml]) can cream of chicken soup, feel free to use low-sodium or Campbell's Healthy Request

2 cups (322 g) cooked rice

½ cup (63 g) sliced almonds

½ cup (118 ml) mayonnaise

2 stalks celery, diced

2 cups (56 g) corn flakes, crushed

2 tbsp (29 g) butter, melted

Preheat the oven to 350°F (177°C).

Combine all ingredients, except for the corn flakes and butter, in a lightly greased 9" x 13" (23 x 33 cm) baking dish. Make sure to mix all ingredients thoroughly, right in the baking dish.

Sprinkle the crushed corn flakes on top of the casserole and drizzle the melted butter.

Bake for 30 to 40 minutes, or until the casserole is heated through. Allow to cool for a few minutes before serving.

This casserole is excellent for lunch the following day should you have any leftovers.

LOADED BAKED POTATO CASSEROLE

YIELD: 10 SERVINGS

I took one of the most popular recipes on my blog, Twice-Baked Potato Casserole, added some chicken and broccoli and turned it into a meal!

If you are looking for a comfort food recipe that will feed a crowd, look no further. This casserole has all the flavors of a twice-baked potato, but in casserole form. It's cheesy, gooey and packed full of flavor, so be prepared for your family to clean their plates!

5 lbs (2.3 kg) red potatoes

½ cup (115 g) butter

16 oz (889 ml) sour cream

8 oz (227 g) cream cheese

1 tsp salt

1 tsp fresh ground black pepper

1 tsp paprika

1 tsp garlic powder

12 oz (340 g) broccoli florets, cooked to crisp-tender

1 rotisserie chicken, skin removed, chopped

8 slices bacon, cooked and crumbled

8 oz (227 g) shredded cheese, cheddar, Mexican blend or Monterey Jack all work

OPTIONAL TOPPING

4 oz (113 g) shredded cheese

Preheat the oven to 350°F (177°C).

Grease a deep 9" x 13" (23 x 33 cm) casserole dish with nonstick cooking spray and set aside.

Boil the potatoes until fork-tender, making sure to generously salt the water while cooking. Mash the boiled potatoes with butter, sour cream, cream cheese, salt, pepper, paprika and garlic powder. Taste the potatoes and add additional seasoning, if needed, before moving on.

Stir in the remaining ingredients and transfer to the prepared casserole dish. Top with additional cheese if desired.

Bake for 25 to 30 minutes, or until heated through. Enjoy!

CHEESY CHICKEN, BROCCOLI AND RICE CASSEROLE

YIELD: 6 SERVINGS

This is one of the most popular recipes on my blog, and it's the casserole that you want to make tonight. Melted cheese, chunks of chicken and tender broccoli are the perfect companions in this comforting one-dish meal. The crunchy corn flake topping is the perfect finishing touch! What else? This casserole is a great way to get your kids to eat their veggies!

3 cups (375 g) diced rotisserie chicken

3 cups (687 g) broccoli florets, broken down into bite-size pieces

1 (10 ¾ oz [305 ml]) can cream of chicken soup, feel free to use low-sodium or Campbell's Healthy Request

2 cups (322 g) cooked rice

8 oz (227 g) shredded cheddar cheese

½ cup (118 ml) mayonnaise

2 cups (56 g) corn flakes, crushed

2 tbsp (29 g) butter, melted

Preheat the oven to 350°F (177°C).

Combine all of the ingredients, except for the corn flakes and butter, right in your baking dish (fewer dishes to wash, you're welcome).

Sprinkle the crushed corn flakes over the casserole and drizzle the melted butter.

Bake for 30 to 35 minutes, or until the casserole is heated through.

NOTE: I use a 9" x 13" (23 x 33 cm) baking dish for this recipe because my family likes the extra surface space for the corn flakes (more crunch!). But this recipe will also fit into an 8" x 8" (20 x 20 cm) or 9" x 9" (23 x 23 cm) baking dish.

CHICKEN CORDON BLEU PASTA CASSEROLE

YIELD: 8 SERVINGS

Casseroles are my favorite type of comfort food. I especially love this recipe because it's inspired by my all-time favorite dish: chicken cordon bleu. My mom used to make chicken cordon bleu for Christmas, and it was the meal I requested every year on my birthday. This casserole has all the great flavors of the classic but takes no time at all to prepare. It captures the essence and richness of chicken cordon bleu, while eliminating all the pounding, rolling and toothpicks. Cheesy, filling and delicious—I think you'll find this dish to be the perfect comfort food!

¼ cup (57 g) butter

1 (10 ¾ oz [305 ml]) can cream of chicken soup, feel free to use low-sodium or Campbell's Healthy Request

⅔ cup (158 ml) evaporated milk

⅓ cup (79 ml) white wine

8 oz (227 g) grated Swiss cheese

1 tbsp (15 ml) Dijon mustard, optional

¼ tsp ground white pepper

1 lb (454 g) penne pasta, cooked

3 cups (375 g) diced rotisserie chicken

8 oz (227 g) cooked, cubed ham

FOR THE TOPPING

3 tbsp (43 g) butter, melted

1 cup (121 g) panko bread crumbs

¼ tsp paprika

1 tsp dried parsley

Preheat the oven to 350°F (177°C). Spray a 9" x 13" (23 x 33 cm) baking dish with nonstick cooking spray. Then, set aside.

Melt the butter over medium heat in a large saucepan. Stir in the cream of chicken soup, evaporated milk and white wine. Continue stirring until the mixture is completely combined, about 2 minutes.

Whisk in the cheese and continue stirring until completely melted, about 2 to 3 minutes. Now it's time to stir in the Dijon mustard and ground white pepper. If you don't like Dijon mustard, it's okay to omit it from this recipe—no biggie! Remove the cheese sauce from the heat.

In a large bowl or pot, combine the cheese sauce, cooked pasta, chicken and ham. You can even dump everything directly into your baking dish like I usually do (because I'm lazy). Stir well to evenly coat all ingredients—you want the cheesy goodness throughout the entire casserole. Pour into the prepared baking dish, if you didn't use my lazy method.

Now it's time for the topping. Combine the melted butter, panko, paprika and parsley in a small bowl. Stir until the panko is evenly coated with butter and the seasonings. It'll turn a nice golden color once mixed.

Sprinkle the topping evenly over the casserole. Bake, uncovered, for 22 to 25 minutes, or until the sauce is bubbling and the topping is golden brown. Allow casserole to set for 5 minutes before serving. Enjoy!

NOTE: Chicken stock or broth can easily be substituted for the wine. The overall flavor will change a bit, but not substantially.

CHICKEN AND SPINACH NOODLE CASSEROLE

YIELD: 8 SERVINGS

I adore the layered look of this casserole; it is so pretty and the presentation is always spot-on. You can see the creamy white layer directly underneath the cheddar cheese and the bright green spinach peeking out. Your family will dive right on into this hearty casserole!

1 tbsp (15 ml) olive oil

1 small onion, diced

16 oz (454 g) tomato sauce

1 tsp Italian seasoning

½ tsp garlic powder

½ tsp salt

½ tsp fresh ground black pepper

2 ½ cups (397 g) shredded rotisserie chicken

8 oz (445 ml) sour cream

8 oz (227 g) cream cheese, softened

1 egg, at room temperature

½ cup (118 ml) milk

8 oz (227 g) wide egg noodles, cooked according to package directions

10 oz (283 g) frozen spinach, thawed and squeezed dry

4 oz (113 g) shredded cheddar cheese

Preheat the oven to 350°F (177°C).

Heat the olive oil in a large skillet over medium heat. Add the onion and cook, stirring frequently, until onion is soft and translucent, about 4 to 5 minutes.

Add the tomato sauce, Italian seasoning, garlic powder and salt and pepper. Bring to a simmer and continue cooking for 6 to 7 minutes. Stir in the shredded chicken and continue simmering for an additional 2 minutes. Remove from heat and set aside.

Add the sour cream and cream cheese to the bowl of a mixer and beat until thoroughly combined and smooth. Add the egg and milk and beat until combined.

Spray a 3-quart (3-L) baking dish with nonstick cooking spray. Layer the noodles, chicken mixture, spinach and the cream cheese mixture. Cover with foil and bake in the preheated oven for 40 minutes.

Remove the foil and sprinkle the cheddar cheese over the casserole. Return to the oven and bake uncovered for an additional 10 to 15 minutes, or until the cheese is melted. Allow the casserole to rest for 5 minutes before serving.

CHICKEN POT PIE

YIELD: 6 SERVINGS

My husband loves, and I really mean LOVES, chicken pot pie. This filling is super similar to the one in my Chicken and Buttermilk Dumplings (page 209) recipe, and it's equally amazing. I'm partial to puff pastry, so I ditched the classic pie crust in favor of the buttery, flaky pastry topping. You can thank me later.

You'll notice that I cut the pastry into rounds. This makes serving time a lot easier as you don't have to deal with "breaking" the crust. I also think it's pretty darn cute.

3 tbsp (43 g) unsalted butter

1 onion, diced

1 stalk celery, diced

2 carrots, diced

½ tsp salt

½ tsp fresh ground black pepper

⅓ cup (42 g) all-purpose flour

2 cups (473 ml) low-sodium chicken broth

6 oz (170 g) green beans, cut into thirds

2 cups (250 g) diced rotisserie chicken

1 sheet frozen puff pastry, thawed

1 egg, lightly beaten

Preheat the oven to 375°F (191°C).

Melt the butter in a large pan over medium-high heat. Add the onion, celery and carrots and season with the salt and pepper. Cook for 5 to 6 minutes, or until the onion is soft and translucent.

Add in the flour and cook for an additional minute, stirring frequently.

Gradually add in the chicken broth, stirring constantly. Bring the mixture to a boil and then reduce the heat to low and simmer for about 5 minutes.

Remove from the heat and stir in the green beans and chicken. Transfer the mixture to a 9-inch (23-cm) pie plate. Then, set aside.

Place the thawed puff pastry on a cutting board and cut out rounds with a biscuit cutter. Place the rounds on top of the filling and brush the puff pastry with the beaten egg.

Bake for 30 to 35 minutes, or until the puff pastry is golden brown and the filling is bubbling. Serve immediately.

NOTE: If you saved the drippings from the rotisserie chicken (page 8), add them at the same time as the broth.

*See picture on page 10.

CHICKEN TETRAZZINI

YIELD: 8 SERVINGS

Wowza! Your new favorite casserole is right HERE. I adapted this recipe from my Aunt Lana's Turkey Tetrazzini, and let me tell you, it's absolutely delightful! Peppers, onions, mushrooms and juicy rotisserie chicken in a cheesy sauce—YUM! My boys love the familiarity of the spaghetti, and who can resist a cheese sauce? You can add more or less veggies to suit your family's preferences, but definitely give this one a try.

½ cup (115 g) butter

1 medium onion, diced

1 green bell pepper, diced

8 oz (227 g) mushrooms, sliced

1 tsp salt

½ tsp fresh ground black pepper

¼ cup (31 g) all-purpose flour

1 chicken bouillon cube

1 cup (237 ml) chicken broth

4 cups (946 ml) milk

16 oz (454 g) shredded Monterey Jack cheese, divided

1 rotisserie chicken, skin removed, shredded

16 oz (454 g) spaghetti, cooked

Preheat the oven to 350°F (177°C).

Grease a deep 9" x 13" (23 x 33 cm) casserole dish with nonstick cooking spray and set aside.

Heat the butter in a large skillet over medium-high heat. Sauté the onion, bell pepper and mushrooms for 4 to 5 minutes, or until the onion is soft and translucent. Season with salt and pepper.

Stir in the flour and bouillon cube. Gradually whisk in the broth and milk and bring to a simmer. Simmer, whisking frequently, for about 4 to 6 minutes, or until the sauce has thickened.

Add in ¾ of the cheese and stir until melted. Stir in the chicken and cooked spaghetti. Transfer the mixture to the prepared casserole dish and top with the remaining cheese.

Bake for 30 to 35 minutes, or until heated through and the cheese is golden and bubbling. Enjoy!

NOTE: Heating the chicken broth and milk prior to adding them to the skillet will speed up the process greatly.

CORNBREAD TACO BAKE

YIELD: 6 SERVINGS

There's not much I like more than warm cornbread drizzled with butter and honey . . . I can't get enough of it! I love it even more in this recipe. This casserole has a Mexican twist with an unconventional topping—cornbread and French fried onions. And cheese. Don't forget the cheese! If you're looking for a hearty, crowd-pleasing dinner, this casserole won't disappoint!

1 tbsp (15 ml) extra virgin olive oil

½ green bell pepper, diced

2 cups (250 g) diced rotisserie chicken

½ cup (118 ml) water

1 tbsp (9 g) taco seasoning

1 (15 ¼ oz [432 g]) can sweet corn, drained

1 (15 oz [425 g]) can black beans, rinsed and drained

1 (8 oz [227 g]) can tomato sauce

1 (8 ½ oz [240 g]) package corn muffin mix + ingredients to prepare it

4 oz (113 g) French fried onions, divided

4 oz (113 g) shredded cheddar cheese

Preheat the oven to 400°F (205°C).

Lightly spray a 2-quart (7-L) casserole dish with nonstick cooking spray and set aside.

Heat the olive oil in a medium sauté pan over medium-high heat and sauté the green pepper for 2 to 3 minutes.

Add the chicken, water, taco seasoning, corn, beans and tomato sauce to the pan and cook for about 5 minutes, stirring frequently. Remove from the heat and set aside.

Prepare the corn muffin mix according to the package instructions and stir in half of the French fried onions into the batter.

Pour the chicken mixture into the prepared dish and spread the cornbread batter on top. Bake for 20 minutes, or until the cornbread topping is golden brown.

Top the casserole with the remaining onions and shredded cheese. Bake for another 3 to 5 minutes, or until the cheese has melted.

Remove the casserole from the oven and allow it to rest for several minutes before serving.

POTATO CHIP CASSEROLE

YIELD: 8 SERVINGS

If you're looking for a casserole that your kids won't say no to, this is the one to try! Casseroles are good-for-the-soul food, but they can also be kid-friendly, like this one. Topped with chips and cheese, this casserole is impossible to resist!

1 tbsp (15 ml) olive oil

1 medium onion, diced

2 cloves garlic, minced

2 cups (250 g) diced rotisserie chicken

½ cup (118 ml) mayonnaise

3 stalks celery, diced

1 (10 ¾ oz [305 ml]) can cream of chicken soup

2 cups (322 g) cooked rice

1 (8 oz [227 g]) can sliced water chestnuts, drained and diced

8 oz (227 g) shredded cheddar cheese, divided

4 oz (114 g) crushed potato chips

Preheat the oven to 350°F (177°C). Spray a 9" x 13" (23 x 33 cm) baking dish with nonstick cooking spray.

Heat the olive oil over medium heat in a medium sauté pan. Sauté the diced onion for 4 to 5 minutes, or until it is soft and translucent. Add the garlic and sauté for an additional minute.

Combine the sautéed onion and garlic with the chicken, mayonnaise, celery, cream of chicken soup, rice, water chestnuts and about half of the shredded cheese in a large bowl. Mix well and transfer to the prepared baking dish.

Sprinkle the remaining cheese and potato chips on top. Bake for 30 minutes, or until the cheese topping is completely melted. Serve and enjoy!

MINI PESTO AND BACON CASSEROLES

YIELD: 4 SERVINGS

Everything is cuter when it's little, and that is especially true with food. These mini casseroles are packed full of flavor and are *oh-so fun*! Pesto, bacon, cheese and chicken—how could we go wrong?

12 oz (340 g) rigatoni OR any other tubular pasta, cooked and drained

2 cups (250 g) diced rotisserie chicken

1 cup (240 g) refrigerated pesto

8 oz (227 g) shredded mozzarella cheese

8 oz (227 g) bacon, cooked and crumbled

2 tbsp (29 g) butter, melted

½ cup (60 g) panko bread crumbs

1 tbsp (3 g) minced fresh parsley

Preheat the oven to 350°F (177°C). Spray four 12-oz (340-g) ramekins with nonstick cooking spray and set aside. Combine pasta, chicken, pesto, cheese and bacon in a large bowl and stir until pesto has been evenly distributed.

Spoon the filling evenly into each of the prepared ramekins. If you have a little extra, no problem, just fill another ramekin with it.

Combine the butter, panko and parsley in a small bowl. Sprinkle some of the topping over the pasta in each ramekin.

Place the ramekins on a baking sheet (this makes removing them from the oven a breeze), and bake for 25 minutes, or until the cheese is melted and the panko is golden brown.

Carefully remove from the oven and serve. If you have small children, let the ramekins cool for a bit and then warn everyone that the dishes are HOT. Safety first, please!

NOTE: If your panko is not cooperating and refuses to turn a golden brown, pop the ramekins under the broiler for a few minutes to get that pretty color.

OVERNIGHT CRAN-APPLE CHICKEN STUFFING CASSEROLE

YIELD: 6 SERVINGS

Stuffing is NOT just for Thanksgiving and Christmas. I love it in this overnight casserole! Granny Smith apples and dried cranberries add a fruity flavor and an amazing texture. This is such a simple meal to put together the night before, and all you have to do is throw it in the oven when you get home from work the next day—it doesn't get any easier!

3 cups (375 g) diced rotisserie chicken

1 (10 ½ oz [298 g]) can cream of mushroom soup

1 (10 ¾ oz [308 g]) can cream of chicken soup

6 oz (170 g) herb stuffing

½ cup (115 g) butter

1 ½ cups (355 ml) low-sodium chicken broth OR stock

2 Granny Smith apples, cored and chopped

¾ cup (114 g) dried cranberries

3 oz (85 g) French fried onions

Lightly spray a 9″ x 13″ (23 x 33 cm) baking dish with nonstick cooking spray.

Combine all ingredients, except for the French fried onions, in a large bowl. Transfer the mixture to the prepared baking dish and cover with foil. Refrigerate overnight.

When you are ready to bake, preheat the oven to 350°F (177°C). Remove the foil and sprinkle the casserole with the French fried onions, leaving it at room temperature while the oven preheats. Bake casserole for 45 to 60 minutes, or until thoroughly heated through. Serve immediately.

CHEESY CHICKEN, POTATO AND GREEN BEAN CASSEROLE

YIELD: 8 SERVINGS

This recipe reminds me a lot of Thanksgiving for some reason. I guess it's the "green beans" and the "casserole" together in the title. I started with one of my favorite breakfast casserole recipes and turned it into the most amazing dinner.

Chicken and potatoes go together like bread and butter, and the evidence is right here in this casserole. The green beans are the perfect addition, and we all know everything is better with cheese. This homey dish is what your kids will be requesting for dinner night after night!

16 oz (889 ml) sour cream

1 (10 ¾ oz [305 g]) can cream of chicken soup, feel free to use low-sodium

12 oz (340 g) fresh green beans, cooked to crisp-tender and cut into 1″ (2.5 cm) pieces

30 oz (850 g) frozen hash brown potatoes

2 tsp (10 g) salt

1 tsp fresh ground black pepper

1 tsp garlic powder

1 shallot, diced

8 oz (227 g) shredded Mexican blend cheese

3 cups (375 g) diced rotisserie chicken

1 (4 oz [113 g]) sleeve Ritz crackers, crushed

1 tbsp (14 g) butter, melted

Preheat the oven to 350°F (177°C).

Grease a deep 9″ x 13″ (23 x 33 cm) casserole dish with nonstick cooking spray and set aside.

Combine all the ingredients, except for the crackers and the butter, in a large bowl. Stir until everything has been evenly distributed.

Transfer to the prepared casserole dish. Sprinkle the crackers over the top of the casserole and drizzle the butter on top.

Bake for 45 to 50 minutes. Serve and enjoy!

NOTE: Leftover turkey would also be great in this recipe!

CHAPTER 2

5 INGREDIENTS OR LESS

This chapter is proof that great meals don't require a lot of ingredients! Tell me if this sounds familiar: You get home and walk to the fridge, but there's not much in there. You walk over to the pantry, same result. You need a recipe that doesn't require a ton of ingredients and that you can make in a hurry AND that your family will love. Sound familiar? That's my life.

Good news! I've got some great recipes here that need only five ingredients, or less, to make. Be sure to try these tried-and-true kid-pleasers: BBQ Chicken Loaded Baked Potatoes (page 35), Ravioli Skillet Lasagna (page 42) and Chicken Teriyaki Stir-Fry (page 46).

BBQ CHICKEN LOADED BAKED POTATOES

YIELD: 4 SERVINGS

I first started making this recipe when I was in college. It was a meal that I could prepare with just a microwave, and it's pretty darn inexpensive to boot. You need only a handful of ingredients for a wonderfully tasty dinner. Once I got married, it quickly became a staple in our home—and I know you're going to love it too!

4 large baking potatoes

2 cups (250 g) shredded rotisserie chicken

⅓ cup (80 ml) barbecue sauce

4 oz (113 g) shredded cheddar cheese

½ cup (118 ml) sour cream, optional

Sliced green onions, optional

Bacon bits, optional

Preheat the oven to 400°F (205°C).

Using a fork, poke several holes in the potatoes. Microwave for 8 to 12 minutes on high until fork-tender.

Combine the shredded chicken and barbecue sauce in a small bowl. Then, set aside.

Split the potatoes down the center and fluff the flesh of the potato with a fork. Divide the chicken mixture evenly among the four potatoes and top with the shredded cheese.

Place the potatoes on a baking sheet and bake until the cheese has melted, about 8 to 10 minutes.

Top with sour cream, green onions and bacon bits, if desired.

NOTE: If you prefer to bake the potatoes, poke some holes in them with a fork and drizzle some olive oil on top. Sprinkle each potato with kosher salt and place on a baking sheet. Bake at 400°F (205°C) for about 1 hour, or until nice and crispy. The oil and salt make for a tasty potato with a super crispy skin.

The cheese can also be melted in the microwave. Just pop in the microwave at high power for 1 to 2 minutes, or until the cheese is fully melted.

SKILLET CHICKEN CHILAQUILES

YIELD: 6 SERVINGS

Chilaquiles are traditionally served for breakfast or brunch with a fried egg on top. The tortillas are also fried now that I think of it. There's so much frying going on that it makes me tired just thinking about it!

This version of chilaquiles is perfect for dinner, and it couldn't be easier or more scrumptious. Tortilla chips are coated in salsa verde, topped with cheese and placed under the broiler so the cheese can get perfectly melted and the chips get beautifully crisp around the edges.

Feel free to eat it as it is, or to top it with avocado, sour cream (or Mexican crema), diced tomatoes, cilantro, green onions or black olives. It's truly amazing!

16 oz (467 ml) salsa verde

1 cup (240 ml) low-sodium chicken broth

2 cups (250 g) shredded rotisserie chicken

8 oz (213 g) tortilla chips

8 oz (227 g) shredded Monterey Jack cheese

OPTIONAL TOPPINGS

Avocado

Sour cream

Diced tomatoes

Cilantro

Sliced green onions

Black olives

Preheat the oven broiler.

Heat the salsa and chicken broth in an oven-safe skillet over medium-high heat until simmering. Stir in the chicken and continue cooking, stirring frequently, until the chicken is heated through, about 5 minutes.

Add in the chips, a handful at a time, tossing to coat. You want the chips to be thoroughly covered with the salsa. Once all of the chips have been added, top with the shredded cheese and place the entire skillet under the broiler for 3 to 5 minutes, or until the cheese is melted and bubbling. Remove the skillet from the oven and top with whatever toppings you like, or serve as is.

CHICKEN CORDON BLEU CRESCENT ROLLS

YIELD: 4 SERVINGS

This is one of three chicken cordon bleu recipes in this book. There's a really simple reason for that: The ingredients just work together so well! This recipe is actually from my blog, and it's a crowd favorite to be sure. It's one of those recipes that just WORKS. A can of crescent rolls, chicken, ham, Swiss cheese and Italian seasoning ensure a quick and painless dinner that's bursting with flavor. This recipe is just the perfect way to utilize rotisserie chicken in a delicious, easy meal that the whole family will love!

1 (8 oz [226 g]) can refrigerated crescent rolls

1 tsp Italian seasoning

6 slices Swiss cheese

6 slices deli ham

2 rotisserie chicken breasts, thinly sliced

2 tbsp (30 ml) honey, optional

2 tbsp (30 ml) Dijon mustard, optional

Preheat the oven to 375°F (191°C). Lightly spray a pie pan or 9" x 9" (23 x 23 cm) baking dish with nonstick cooking spray. Then, set aside.

Remove the crescent rolls from the can and lay the dough out in a long rectangle. Pinch the seams together well; you're not going to tear them apart like you normally would. Sprinkle the top of the dough with the Italian seasoning, then layer the cheese, ham and finally, the chicken.

Starting on the longer side, roll the dough up like a cinnamon roll and cut into eight rolls. Place in the prepared baking dish and bake for 18 to 20 minutes, or until golden brown.

If you'd like, whisk together the honey and Dijon mustard and serve with the hot rolls. Delish!

CHICKEN JALAPEÑO POPPER PINWHEELS

YIELD: 8 PINWHEELS

Time to spice up dinner! Inspired by one of my favorite appetizers—jalapeño poppers—these easy-to-make pinwheels use only four ingredients. FOUR! A mixture of cream cheese, jalapeños and diced chicken is spread onto crescent roll dough and rolled up like cinnamon rolls. Baked until golden brown, the cream cheese filling is mind-blowingly delicious. Now you can have appetizers for dinner!

8 oz (227 g) cream cheese, softened (feel free to substitute light cream cheese)

1 cup (125 g) diced rotisserie chicken

1 to 2 jalapeños, seeded, deveined and diced

1 (8 oz [226 g]) can refrigerated crescent rolls

Preheat the oven to 375°F (191°C).

Lightly spray a pie pan or 9" x 9" (23 x 23 cm) baking dish with nonstick cooking spray.

In a small bowl, combine the softened cream cheese, chicken and jalapeños and mix until thoroughly combined. Then, set aside.

Remove the crescent rolls from the can and lay the dough out in a long rectangle. Pinch the seams together well; you're not going to tear them apart like you normally would.

Gently spread the cream cheese mixture on the dough. Starting on the longer side, roll it up like a cinnamon roll, pinching the end seams together. Cut into eight rolls.

Place the rolls in the prepared baking dish and bake for 20 to 22 minutes, or until golden brown. Allow pinwheels to cool for 2 to 3 minutes before enjoying.

CHICKEN NACHOS SUPREME

YIELD: 6 SERVINGS

Nachos: appetizer turned dinner in the best way possible. Quite possibly the EASIEST recipe in this book, these nachos are just too good not to include.

Happy dances are not an uncommon occurrence when my boys hear that Chicken Nachos Supreme is what's on the menu for dinner. I'm secretly dancing my own happy dance inside because I love making this simple recipe that's packed with flavor for my family.

I serve the nachos family style and let the kids serve themselves. All the toppings are on the table so everyone can make his or her nachos just the way they like them!

12 oz (340 g) tortilla chips

2 cups (250 g) shredded rotisserie chicken

1 (16 oz [454 g]) can pinto beans, rinsed and drained

8 oz (227 g) shredded Mexican blend cheese

½ cup (122 g) pico de gallo salsa

OPTIONAL TOPPINGS

Sour cream

Guacamole or sliced avocado

Cilantro

Diced tomatoes

Salsa, any kind you like

Pickled jalapeños

Preheat the oven to 425°F (218°C).

Line a rimmed baking sheet with foil. Layer half of the chips on the baking sheet and top with half of the chicken, beans and cheese. Repeat with the remaining halves.

Bake nachos for 10 to 12 minutes, or until the cheese is melted and bubbling. Top with pico de gallo and any additional toppings you desire and serve immediately.

RAVIOLI SKILLET LASAGNA

YIELD: 6 SERVINGS

This recipe is easy, cheesy and over-the-top comfort food all done in a single skillet. I picked up some spinach and cheese ravioli for this recipe and it was perfection, but feel free to use your favorite type here. My favorite part about this dish is the look and texture the cheese gets from being broiled.

If I happen to have some fresh basil on hand, I like to sprinkle it right on top of the entire skillet lasagna. It adds a bit of elegance to this otherwise homey dish.

20 oz (567 g) refrigerated ravioli, I used spinach and cheese ravioli

1 (24 oz [680 g]) jar marinara or pasta sauce

8 oz (227 g) shredded mozzarella cheese

2 cups (250 g) shredded rotisserie chicken

2 oz (57 g) grated Parmesan cheese

Fresh basil for garnish, optional

Preheat the oven broiler.

Fill a large, deep oven-safe skillet with water and cook the ravioli according to the package directions. Drain and remove from the skillet. Then, set aside.

Add about a third of the marinara sauce to the bottom of the skillet and top with half of the cooked ravioli. Sprinkle about half of the shredded cheese on top, followed by the chicken. Pour another third of the marinara sauce directly over the chicken. Top with remaining ravioli, marinara sauce, mozzarella and Parmesan cheese.

Place skillet under the broiler for 4 to 5 minutes, or until the cheese is golden and bubbling. Garnish with fresh basil, if desired.

CHICKEN PARMESAN CALZONES

YIELD: 6 CALZONES

You've gotta love these five-ingredient recipes! This one in particular is one of my favorites because I'm a chicken Parmesan-aholic. The good news is my family loves it too, so they don't get sick of me making it all the time.

I love this twist on the classic. All those delectable flavors together inside a pizza dough crust are just fantastic! Serve with a crisp garden salad for the perfect meal!

¾ cup (177 ml) marinara sauce

2 cups (250 g) shredded rotisserie chicken

1 lb (454 g) pizza dough

8 oz (227 g) shredded mozzarella cheese

4 oz (113 g) shredded Parmesan cheese, divided

Olive oil, to brush the calzones with

Preheat the oven to 425°F (218°C).

Combine the marinara sauce and chicken in a medium bowl and stir to combine. Then, set aside.

Divide the pizza dough into six equal portions and roll them out into 6-inch (15-cm) circles.

Divide even amounts of the chicken mixture among the six dough circles. Make sure to spoon the chicken mixture onto the center of each dough circle, leaving the borders clean. Sprinkle the mozzarella cheese and half of the Parmesan on top of the chicken. Fold the dough over the filling and pinch the edges together to seal it.

Slice two steam vents into the top of the calzones and then brush with olive oil. Sprinkle each calzone with the remaining Parmesan cheese.

Bake for 12 to 15 minutes, or until golden brown.

CHICKEN TERIYAKI STIR-FRY

YIELD: 6 SERVINGS

Stir-fries are a great way to incorporate tons of veggies into your dinner without a lot of fuss. This recipe uses a bag of frozen stir-fry blend veggies and store-bought teriyaki sauce for loads of convenience. Make sure to buy high-quality teriyaki sauce for exceptional flavor. This is a recipe where the entire family ends up licking their bowls clean!

2 tbsp (30 ml) vegetable oil

1 (12 oz [340 g]) bag frozen stir-fry blend vegetables

2 cups (250 g) diced rotisserie chicken

½ cup (118 ml) teriyaki sauce

Cooked rice, for serving with

Sesame seeds, for garnish (optional)

Heat the vegetable oil in a wok or large skillet over medium-high heat. Add the frozen veggies and cook for 7 to 8 minutes, stirring frequently.

Add the chicken and teriyaki sauce and continue cooking until simmering. Cook for an additional 5 minutes, stirring frequently, or until the chicken is heated through.

We enjoy our stir-fry over steamed rice, but you could also serve it with chow mein or fried rice. Garnish with sesame seeds, if using.

CHILE RELLENO QUESADILLAS

YIELD: 4 SERVINGS

I was talking to my sister on the phone, and she told me about these amazing *chile rellenos* that she and her husband had eaten for dinner. My stomach started growling.

I quickly thought of a simple solution. These quesadillas are a great way to get all that chile and cheese yumminess in a quick and tasty tortilla package. The perfect easy dinner!

2 cups (250 g) shredded rotisserie chicken

1 (4 oz [113 g]) can diced green chiles, drained

8 oz (227 g) shredded Monterey Jack cheese

2 tbsp (30 ml) vegetable oil

4 flour tortillas, burrito size

Combine the shredded chicken, green chiles and cheese in a small bowl. Stir to combine and set aside.

Drizzle the vegetable oil over a large skillet at medium-high heat.

I am a total klutz when it comes to flipping tortillas, so I use the fold method instead. Lay a tortilla on the hot oil and spread the chicken filling on one HALF of the tortilla. Gently fold the other half over the top of the filling.

Grill the tortilla for 3 to 4 minutes, or until golden brown, and carefully flip over. The good news is that you can only lose filling out of one side now. Grill the other side for another few minutes just until golden brown. Cut into wedges and serve!

CHEESY BUFFALO CHICKEN ALFREDO BAKE

YIELD: 6 SERVINGS

This recipe doesn't have a whole lot of ingredients, but what it does have is a whole lot of flavor! The heat from the buffalo sauce is perfectly matched by the creamy, decadent Alfredo sauce. Use your favorite pasta (i.e., whatever you can find in your pantry) for this dish. Penne, rotini, rigatoni and even macaroni would be excellent!

¼ cup (59 ml) buffalo sauce

2 cups (250 g) diced rotisserie chicken

1 (15 oz [425 g]) jar Alfredo sauce

8 oz (227 g) shredded mozzarella cheese

16 oz (454 g) pasta, cooked

Preheat the oven to 350°F (177°C).

Combine the buffalo sauce and chicken in a small bowl. Then, set side.

Combine the Alfredo sauce, about 3 ounces (85 g) of the cheese and the cooked pasta in a large bowl. Then, set aside.

Lightly grease a 2- or 3-quart (2- or 3-L) baking dish with nonstick cooking spray.

Spoon half of the pasta mixture into the bottom of the baking dish, top with the chicken mixture and then the other half of the pasta mixture. Sprinkle the remaining cheese on top.

Cover with foil and bake for 30 minutes. Then remove the foil and bake for 5 to 10 more minutes, or until the cheese is bubbling.

Remove from the oven and allow to rest for several minutes before serving.

BBQ CHICKEN NACHOS CRESCENT BRAID

YIELD: 6 SERVINGS

This one's for the nacho-loving family! I'm pretty sure my boys would happily live on nachos should the occasion ever arise. My husband, too. That's why this BBQ Chicken Nachos Crescent Braid is such a big hit with them.

Sure, they're impressed with the presentation, but they're MUCH more impressed with the bold flavor and cheesy goodness that resides inside this golden crescent package.

½ cup (118 ml) barbecue sauce

2 cups (250 g) shredded rotisserie chicken

1 (8 oz [226 g]) can refrigerated crescent rolls OR seamless crescent roll dough

1 cup (237 ml) salsa con queso OR nacho cheese sauce

Pickled jalapeño slices, optional

Preheat the oven to 350°F (177°C).

Combine the barbecue sauce and chicken in a medium bowl and stir to combine. Then, set aside.

Line a large baking sheet with parchment paper.

Open the crescent roll can and carefully lay out the dough onto the parchment-lined sheet. Pinch the seams together to create one large piece of crescent dough, if using dough with seams.

On the two long sides, use a sharp knife to cut 2-inch (5-cm) slits every inch (2.5 cm) along the edge. There should be one solid 3-inch (7.6-cm) piece of dough down the center.

Spoon the chicken mixture down the center of the dough, making sure to steer clear of the edges. Spoon the nacho sauce on top and sprinkle with pickled jalapeño slices—if you can handle the heat.

Starting on one end, fold one strip up and over the filling. Go to the other side and pull one strip up and over the filling from that side. Continue pulling the strips over the filling, alternating sides as you move down the length of dough, until all strips have been crossed over the dough. Pinch the dough together at both ends of the crescent braid to keep the filling from spilling out.

Bake for 20 to 25 minutes, or until golden brown. Cut into slices and serve.

CHAPTER 3

20-MINUTE DINNERS

I think we can all agree that a few extra hours in the day would be greatly appreciated. I don't know what happens in the afternoons, but dinnertime can sure sneak up on me!

I love having an arsenal of 20-minute dinners that I can turn to and that I know my family will enjoy. And by enjoy, I mean scrape those plates clean!

Make sure to try the California Burritos with Cilantro-Lime Rice (page 58), Easy, Cheesy Chicken Fettuccine Alfredo (page 65) and the Sweet and Sour Chicken (page 74).

CLASSIC CHICKEN CAESAR SALAD

YIELD: 6 SERVINGS

There's nothing like a classic chicken Caesar salad! I have found through trial and error that the trick to getting my boys to eat salad—any salad—is croutons. They're like magic on top of a salad. I added liberal amounts of croutons to this recipe, and I have to say that the savory crunch is one of my favorite parts of this salad. Also, please use a good-quality refrigerated Caesar dressing for the best flavor. And use REAL Parmesan cheese—it makes a BIG difference!

1 (10 oz [254 g]) bag hearts of romaine lettuce, already cut

5 oz (142 g) croutons

½ cup (118 ml) refrigerated Caesar dressing

3 oz (85 g) grated Parmesan cheese

2 cups (250 g) diced rotisserie chicken

Combine all ingredients in a large bowl and toss to combine. Serve immediately.

CALIFORNIA BURRITOS WITH CILANTRO-LIME RICE

YIELD: 4 BURRITOS

My family needs an avocado tree to help supplement the enormous amount of avocados we consume each year. Seriously, we can't get enough. I love this burrito recipe because it's so simple and each of the very few ingredients really shines. The cilantro-lime rice is one of our favorites and goes perfectly with black beans and Monterey Jack cheese. The avocado adds a rich creaminess that is truly divine. Enjoy with chips and salsa, and maybe with a margarita or *agua fresca*—yum!

2 cups (322 g) cooked rice

¼ cup (10 g) chopped fresh cilantro

1 lime, juiced

4 flour tortillas, burrito size

1 (15 oz [425 g]) can black beans, rinsed and drained

2 cups (250 g) shredded rotisserie chicken

8 oz (227 g) shredded Monterey Jack cheese

1 avocado, thinly sliced

Preheat the oven to 350°F (177°C).

Combine the rice, cilantro and lime juice in a small bowl. Then, set aside.

Lay a tortilla on a sheet of foil. Layer ¼ of the rice, black beans, chicken, cheese and avocado. Fold the two sides and roll tightly. Wrap the burrito in the foil and set aside. Repeat with the remaining tortillas and fillings.

Place the foil-wrapped burritos on a baking sheet and bake for 10 to 15 minutes, or until the cheese has melted. Serve with chips and salsa!

CHICKEN AND CORNBREAD WAFFLES WITH BALSAMIC MAPLE SYRUP

YIELD: 4 SERVINGS

I hope you're a fan of chicken and waffles! I sure am, and I have to tell you, fried chicken has nothing on rotisserie chicken when it comes to chicken and waffles. I love making cornbread waffles because they have a slightly sweet, but definitely savory, flavor that goes so well with chicken. Try making cornbread waffles to eat alongside chili and soup—so fun! Also, this is the quickest way to make cornbread, hands down. Five minutes in the waffle maker and your cornbread is perfectly cooked and delicious.

I like to break down a whole rotisserie chicken for this recipe; that way, everyone can pick their favorite part. Double the waffle recipe if you'd like; leftovers can be heated in the toaster or toaster oven.

1 cup (240 ml) balsamic vinegar

½ cup (118 ml) maple syrup

1 (8 ½ oz [240 g]) package corn muffin mix

1 egg

½ cup (118 ml) milk

1 rotisserie chicken, broken down

Bring the balsamic vinegar and maple syrup to a simmer in a small saucepan over medium heat. Simmer for 10 to 15 minutes, or until reduced by half. You want it to have a syrup consistency.

Meanwhile, preheat your waffle maker.

Combine the corn muffin mix, egg and milk together in a small bowl. Mix just until combined. Spoon half of the corn muffin mixture into your waffle maker and cook according to the manufacturer's directions. Repeat for the second waffle.

Serve cornbread waffles with pieces of the rotisserie chicken. Drizzle the balsamic maple syrup on top and serve hot.

NOTE: Use the best-quality balsamic vinegar that you can get, and make sure to use REAL maple syrup for best results.

CHICKEN AND SPINACH RAVIOLI

YIELD: 20 RAVIOLI

Homemade ravioli is nothing short of heaven. In a perfect world, I would lovingly make my pasta dough from scratch while listening to Italian music and drinking a glass of wine. My reality, however, is quite a bit different—and that's totally okay. Why? I can still make homemade ravioli and look like the superstar that I am by using a shortcut that no one needs to know about. . . wonton wrappers!

Perfectly suited for ravioli, wonton wrappers are sold in both squares and rounds. Use whichever shape you prefer. The filling is creamy, cheesy and packed with spinach and chicken, making it a hearty meal. Top them with a drizzle of olive oil and a sprinkling of Parmesan cheese or, as my kids prefer, with your favorite pasta sauce. *Mangiamo!*

1 tbsp (15 ml) olive oil

3 cups (121 g) baby spinach

1 cup (125 g) diced rotisserie chicken

1 cup (230 g) ricotta cheese

¾ cup (135 g) grated Parmesan cheese

2 eggs, divided and lightly beaten

Salt and pepper, to taste

1 (12 oz [340 g]) package wonton wrappers, square or round

Heat the olive oil in a medium skillet over medium heat. Add the spinach and cook, stirring frequently, until the spinach has wilted, about 2 to 3 minutes. Remove the spinach and let cool for several minutes. Once cool enough to handle, roughly chop it. Then, set aside.

Fill a large pot with water and bring to a boil. Salt the water to taste.

Combine the diced chicken, ricotta, Parmesan and 1 egg in a medium bowl. Add the salt and pepper to taste. Stir in the chopped spinach until it's thoroughly combined.

Lay the wonton wrappers on a dry, flat surface. Spoon 1 to 2 teaspoons (5 to 10 g) of the filling onto the center of each wrapper. Using a pastry brush, brush the other beaten egg onto the exposed surface of the wonton wrapper, around the filling. Use the egg sparingly—one egg is MORE than enough for the job.

Lay another wrapper on top of the exposed filling. Starting at the center, gently press the top wrapper around the base of the filling, smoothing out to the edges of the wrapper. Be sure to eliminate any air bubbles. Repeat until all filling or wrappers have been used.

Drop four or five ravioli at a time into the salted boiling water. Cook for 3 to 4 minutes before removing with a slotted spoon.

Serve with your favorite pasta sauce or olive oil and Parmesan cheese.

NOTE: These ravioli freeze very well. I like to make a double batch and freeze half. Simply make this recipe up until the point where you cook the ravioli. Place the assembled ravioli in a single layer on a parchment-lined baking sheet and freeze for 45 to 60 minutes. Once frozen, the ravioli can be stored in a freezer storage bag. To cook, place in boiling water for 5 minutes. Easy!

EASY, CHEESY CHICKEN FETTUCCINE ALFREDO

YIELD: 6 SERVINGS

Fettuccine Alfredo has long been a weakness of mine, so knowing how to make it at home is outright dangerous. Especially when it's as easy and delicious as this recipe is! Undeniably rich and luxurious, this dish will cause moans and groans of delight at your dinner table tonight.

½ cup (115 g) butter

1 tsp garlic powder

2 cups (473 ml) heavy cream

5 oz (142 g) grated Parmesan cheese

2 cups (250 g) diced rotisserie chicken

1 lb (454 g) fettuccine pasta, cooked according to package directions

Fresh parsley, chopped, for garnish, if desired

Add the butter and garlic powder to a cold, medium skillet. Cook over medium heat, stirring frequently, until the butter is bubbling.

Add the heavy cream and stir, bringing the mixture to a simmer.

Stir in the Parmesan until the cheese has fully melted and then add the chicken.

Continue cooking over medium heat until the chicken has warmed through, about 5 to 6 minutes.

Stir in the cooked fettuccine and serve immediately.

Garnish with fresh chopped parsley and additional Parmesan cheese, if desired.

NOTE: There are so few ingredients in this recipe that each one plays a critical role. Please use real Parmesan cheese for this recipe. The fake stuff won't melt properly.

MONTEREY CHICKEN PINWHEELS

YIELD: 8 PINWHEELS

Monterey chicken is the most amazing and simple combination of flavors: chicken, cheese, barbecue sauce and bacon. It's utterly delightful.

These pinwheels are the perfect handheld dinner, and they pack a mighty flavorful punch in every bite. Use your favorite barbecue sauce to make it sweet or spicy—your choice!

1 cup (125 g) diced rotisserie chicken

¼ cup (59 ml) barbecue sauce

1 (8 oz [226 g]) can refrigerated crescent rolls

4 oz (113 g) shredded cheddar cheese

4 oz (113 g) shredded Monterey Jack cheese

6 slices bacon, cooked and crumbled

3 green onions, thinly sliced

Preheat the oven to 375°F (191°C).

Lightly spray a pie pan or 9" x 9" (23 x 23 cm) baking dish with nonstick cooking spray.

In a small bowl, combine the chicken and barbecue sauce. Mix until thoroughly combined.

Remove the crescent rolls from the can and lay out the dough in a long rectangle on a lightly floured surface. Pinch the seams together well.

Sprinkle the cheeses evenly on the top of the dough. Next, sprinkle the chicken and bacon.

Starting on the long side of the dough, roll it up like a cinnamon roll. Pinch the ends together and cut into eight rolls. Place the rolls in the prepared baking dish and bake for 20 to 22 minutes, or until golden brown.

Allow rolls to cool for 2 to 3 minutes before removing from the baking dish. Sprinkle with sliced green onions and serve.

PINT-SIZED BBQ CHICKEN PIZZAS

YIELD: 6 SERVINGS

The boys and I make up these mini pizzas for lunch all the time. They're usually *really* fancy, with cheese or maybe cheese *and* pepperoni. You know, the WORKS. However, for dinner we kick it up a notch with these BBQ chicken pizzas. I love the combination of Gouda and mozzarella cheeses, but if you can't find Gouda, go for all mozzarella. You won't be disappointed.

1 (12 ½ oz [354 g]) package English muffins, split

1 tsp Italian seasoning

½ cup (118 ml) barbecue sauce

1 ½ cups (190 g) diced rotisserie chicken

¼ cup (59 ml) pizza sauce

4 oz (113 g) shredded Gouda cheese

½ small red onion, thinly sliced

4 oz (113 g) shredded mozzarella cheese

Fresh cilantro, roughly chopped

Preheat the oven to 400°F (205°C).

Place the split English muffins on a large baking sheet. Sprinkle with the Italian seasoning and pop in the oven for 5 minutes.

Meanwhile, combine the barbecue sauce and chicken in a small bowl, tossing with a fork to evenly coat the chicken. Then, set aside.

Remove the English muffins from the oven and spread a small amount of pizza sauce onto each half.

Sprinkle some Gouda cheese onto each half, then add the chicken, onion and mozzarella cheese. Return the baking sheet to the oven and bake for another 8 to 10 minutes, or until the cheese is melted and bubbling.

Sprinkle with fresh cilantro and serve. Pizza just doesn't get any easier!

PESTO AND SPINACH CHICKEN TORTELLINI SKILLET

YIELD: 6 SERVINGS

One-pot dinners are my FAVORITE. I'm all about keeping the mess to a minimum. My husband would probably disagree with that statement—ha! This tortellini skillet makes use of a number of store-bought items and transforms them into an elegant meal worthy of dinner guests, or hungry kids.

Make sure you buy the refrigerated tortellini—not frozen!

2 tbsp (29 g) unsalted butter

2 tbsp (16 g) all-purpose flour

2 cups (480 ml) low-sodium chicken broth

½ tsp salt

½ tsp fresh ground black pepper

½ cup (118 ml) pesto

20 oz (567 g) refrigerated cheese tortellini

2 cups (250 g) diced rotisserie chicken

2 large handfuls fresh baby spinach

¼ cup (45 g) grated Parmesan cheese

2 oz (57 g) julienned sun-dried tomatoes

Using a large skillet with a lid, melt the butter over medium heat. Whisk in the flour and cook for 1 minute.

Gradually whisk in the broth and bring the mixture to a simmer, and continue simmering for 4 to 5 minutes. Season with the salt and pepper.

Whisk in the pesto and return to a simmer, then add the tortellini and cover.

Simmer for 2 to 3 minutes, stir and cover. Continue cooking for another 2 to 3 minutes, keeping it at a simmer.

Stir in the chicken, spinach, Parmesan cheese and sun-dried tomatoes. It may look like a lot of spinach, but after you stir it, it'll cook down and magically disappear.

Cook on low for another 3 to 4 minutes, or until the chicken is heated through and the spinach has wilted.

Top with additional Parmesan cheese, if desired.

SPICY MANGO CHICKEN

YIELD: 4 SERVINGS

Sometimes I go a little crazy at the grocery store when mangoes are in season. They are just so pretty, and I love having a big bowl of them sitting on the counter—it makes me happy. While eating fresh mangoes is definitely one of my favorite ways to enjoy this tropical fruit, they're also a lot of fun to include in our dinner.

Mangoes are so sweet that they pair beautifully with spicy foods, like habaneros and other chilies. This particular recipe is a perfect example of just how amazing that sweet and spicy combination can be. We enjoy this chicken served over rice or alongside noodles.

3 tbsp (44 ml) honey

¼ cup (59 ml) soy sauce

1 lime, juiced

2 tsp (10 g) chili paste

½ cup (120 ml) mango nectar

2 tsp (6 g) cornstarch

2 cups (250 g) diced rotisserie chicken

1 mango, peeled and diced

½ cup (56 g) roasted and salted cashews

2 green onions, sliced, for garnish

Whisk together the honey, soy sauce, lime juice, chili paste, mango nectar and cornstarch in a small bowl. Add the mixture to a medium skillet and bring to a simmer over medium heat. Continue cooking, stirring frequently, until the sauce thickens, about 3 minutes.

Gently stir in the diced chicken and continue cooking for an additional 5 minutes, or until the chicken is heated through. Stir in the mango and cashews and cook for another 2 to 3 minutes.

Serve over rice or noodles and top with sliced green onions and chopped cashews, if you desire.

NOTE: You can easily increase the heat in this recipe by adding more chili paste or red-pepper chili flakes.

SWEET AND SOUR CHICKEN

YIELD: 6 SERVINGS

If someone had told me 10 years ago how to make sweet and sour sauce at home, I think I would have saved a lot of money eating out at Chinese restaurants over the years. Now that I know how to make my own, there's no turning back.

This sauce is ridiculously easy to make, and it's the BEST sweet and sour sauce I've ever had. If I had to pick five recipes from this book for you to make this week, this would be one of them. It's sweet enough that the kids enjoy it, while the flavors are complex enough for adults. Be done with Chinese takeout and start making it at home . . . tonight!

1 (20 oz [567 g]) can pineapple chunks in 100% juice

½ cup (118 ml) ketchup

1 tbsp (10 g) cornstarch

2 tbsp (30 ml) red wine vinegar

2 tbsp (30 ml) water

1 tbsp (12 g) granulated sugar

1 tbsp (15 ml) vegetable oil

1 red bell pepper, chopped

1 green bell pepper, chopped

½ medium white onion, chopped

3 cups (375 g) diced rotisserie chicken

Cooked rice, to serve with

3 green onions, sliced

Strain the pineapple juice from the can and pour into a medium bowl, reserving the pineapple chunks for later. Whisk in the ketchup, cornstarch, red wine vinegar, water and sugar. Then, set aside.

Heat a wok over medium-high heat. Add the oil, peppers and onion and sauté for 4 to 5 minutes. Remove veggies with a slotted spoon and set aside. Add the sauce to the wok and bring to a simmer, stirring frequently, for about 2 minutes.

Add the chicken, peppers and onion, and the reserved pineapple chunks to the wok, stirring to coat thoroughly with sauce. Cook over medium heat for another 5 to 7 minutes, or until the chicken is heated through.

Serve over steamed rice and top with sliced green onions.

TERIYAKI GINGER POT STICKERS

YIELD: 10 SERVINGS

I have to warn you, these pot stickers are outright addicting. You'll find yourself making these for dinner on Thursday night and then again as appetizers for Saturday's party. The fresh ginger is absolutely essential and really makes these pot stickers pop in your mouth. The filling takes about 5 minutes to prepare, and then it's getting down to business time: filling and folding about 50 of these pot stickers. I usually create an assembly line to ease the process, and if you have older kids who can help, enlist them for goodness' sake! I can't wait until my boys are just a little bit older. . . .

2 cups (250 g) rotisserie chicken, minced

3 green onions, sliced

1 cup (57 g) very thinly sliced Napa cabbage

⅓ cup (79 ml) teriyaki sauce, the thicker the better

2 tsp (10 g) grated fresh ginger

1 (12 oz [340 g]) package round wonton wraps, you may not need all of them

3 tbsp (45 ml) vegetable oil

Combine the chicken, green onions, cabbage, teriyaki sauce and ginger in a medium bowl. Stir together until the teriyaki sauce has been evenly distributed.

Lay out the wonton wraps on a clean, dry surface. They get sticky when wet, so be careful. Spoon about two teaspoons (10 g) of the chicken filling onto the center of each wrap, making sure to leave the edges clean.

Fill a small bowl with water. Dip your finger in the water and run it along the edge of the wonton wrap. Pull the edges together and press together firmly to make sure they are sealed well. You may need to adjust the amount of filling per wonton so not to overfill it. Repeat until you run out of filling.

Now it's time to cook 'em! Heat the oil in a large nonstick skillet. Every time I don't use a nonstick skillet, I kind of regret it. In batches, place the pot stickers in the skillet, seam side up. I like to press down gently so they get a good amount of surface area on the bottom. Don't let the pot stickers touch each other, or they will stick and tear—give them some space. Cook for 2 to 3 minutes, or until golden brown on the bottom. Flip each pot sticker onto its side and cook for an additional 2 to 3 minutes. And then finally, flip to the last side and cook for another 2 to 3 minutes, just until golden brown.

Remove the pot stickers and start the next batch. It took me three rounds to cook them all, and of course, the kids were done eating after the first batch.

Serve warm with additional teriyaki sauce or soy sauce. We enjoy these pot stickers with some rice and chow mein—delicious!

NOTE: You may not need all of the wonton wraps in a package. I had about 9 left over, yielding 51 pot stickers. It will all depend on how much filling you get into each wonton, but anticipate between 40 to 60 pot stickers total.

THAI CHICKEN FLATBREAD PIZZA

YIELD: 4 TO 6 SERVINGS

This is one of my favorite pizzas to order when we're out, but an even bigger favorite at home! I use flatbread or naan to turn this pizza into a super-fast dinner solution, and one that the whole family loves.

There are just so many textures and flavors going on in this pizza—the sweet teriyaki sauce, the crunchy peanut butter, the tender rotisserie chicken and the crisp, fresh veggies. Get in my belly!

½ cup (118 ml) creamy or crunchy peanut butter

⅓ cup (79 ml) teriyaki sauce

2 to 4 pieces flatbread or naan

1 ½ cups (190 g) diced rotisserie chicken

8 oz (227 g) shredded mozzarella cheese

1 carrot, cut into slivers, you can also buy pre-shredded carrots

½ red bell pepper, cut into slivers

3 green onions, sliced

Chopped peanuts, optional

Fresh cilantro for garnish, optional

Preheat the oven to 400°F (205°C).

Combine the peanut butter and teriyaki sauce in a medium microwave-safe bowl and microwave for 30 seconds. Stir until completely combined.

Spread half of the peanut butter mixture onto the flatbreads. Then, set aside.

Add the chicken to the bowl with the remaining peanut butter mixture and stir evenly to coat.

Top the flatbreads with about 5 ounces (142 g) of the cheese. Divide the chicken, carrot, bell pepper and green onions evenly among the pizzas. Top with the remaining cheese and sprinkle the chopped peanuts, if using.

Bake for 10 to 12 minutes, or until the cheese is melted and bubbly. Garnish with additional peanuts and fresh cilantro, if you'd like.

NOTE: You'll notice that I have chopped peanuts listed as an optional garnish in the ingredients list. Considering the prevalence of peanut allergies, I prefer to be safe than sorry. If you're serving up these pizzas to a crowd and garnishing the pizzas with peanuts, tell those with allergies to steer clear.

CHICKEN FRIED RICE

YIELD: 8 SERVINGS

I love it when a side dish can be turned into a meal, and this recipe is a great example. Fried rice is a must when we go out for Chinese food. It's one of our favorite side dishes to enjoy, and we love to make it at home. Adding extra chicken and upping the veggies turns this recipe into a satisfying and delicious dinner.

3 cups (375 g) diced rotisserie chicken

2 tbsp (30 ml) sesame oil, divided

2 tbsp (30 ml) vegetable oil

1 onion, diced

2 carrots, diced

1 clove garlic, minced

3 eggs, lightly beaten

4 cups (644 g) cold rice

12 oz (340 g) frozen peas

2 tbsp (30 ml) soy sauce

2 green onions, sliced (optional)

In a medium bowl, toss the chicken with 1 tablespoon (15 ml) of sesame oil and set aside.

Heat the vegetable oil over high heat in a wok or very large skillet. Add the onion and carrots and stir-fry for 3 to 4 minutes, or until the onion has softened. Stir in the garlic and continue cooking for 1 minute.

Move the veggies to one side of the wok and pour the beaten eggs onto the other side. Continually stir the eggs gently until they are scrambled. Move the eggs to the top of the veggies.

Add the remaining sesame oil to the bottom of the wok and let it heat up for just about 1 minute.

Add the chicken, rice and peas and stir it all together. Add the soy sauce and stir to evenly coat.

Continue cooking for another 3 to 5 minutes, or until the chicken is heated through. Top with the sliced green onions, if desired.

CHAPTER 4

HANDHELD FAVORITES

Having two little boys and one big one means that I make a lot of handheld foods. Whether we're on the run, eating dinner on the patio or settling in to watch a family movie, it seems like handheld foods continually hold mass appeal for my family.

I'll admit that there is a definite "fun factor" to handheld dinners, and I'm all for these easy, delicious dinner options.

Baked Chicken Chimichangas (page 85), Cheesy Chicken Bakes (page 93) and Mexican Pizzas (page 102) should go straight to the top of your to-do list.

BAKED CHICKEN CHIMICHANGAS

YIELD: 8 CHIMICHANGAS

I order a chimichanga 7 out of 10 times when we go out to a Mexican restaurant. That crispy shell filled with cheesy goodness is just too much for me to resist. The crazy thing is, chimichangas are easy to make at home AND you can make them a lot healthier.

When I make chimichangas at home, I like to bake them so that they are all ready at the same time. (Occasionally, I like to eat WITH my family.) It's also a lot easier and less messy. We top ours with shredded lettuce, guacamole and sour cream. Enjoy!

2 ½ cups (315 g) shredded rotisserie chicken

½ cup (118 ml) salsa

8 flour tortillas, burrito size

1 (16 oz [454 g]) can refried beans, you may not need the entire can

4 oz (113 g) shredded Mexican blend cheese

OPTIONAL TOPPINGS

Sour cream

Diced tomatoes

Salsa

Shredded lettuce

Guacamole

Preheat the oven to 450°F (232°C).

Combine the chicken and salsa in a small bowl. Then, set aside.

Lay the tortillas on a flat surface and spread about 2 tablespoons (30 g) of the refried beans on each one. Top with the chicken mixture and cheese, evenly dividing them among the eight tortillas.

Fold up the sides of each tortilla and roll over tightly.

Spray a large baking sheet with nonstick cooking spray. Place the chimichangas on the baking sheet and spray the tops with cooking spray.

Bake for 12 to 14 minutes, or until the tortillas are golden brown and crispy. Remove from the oven and top with your choice of toppings.

CHICKEN BACON RANCH PIZZA CUPS

YIELD: 8 PIZZA CUPS

Ranch, bacon and chicken belong together. I don't know who would argue with that. It's doubly true if you put those ingredients together on a pizza and top it with loads of glorious cheese.

It really can't get any better, unless you made it into pizza cups—perfect for little hands and grown-up appetites. Yes! This is what you want for dinner!

1 ½ cups (190 g) diced rotisserie chicken

¼ cup (59 ml) ranch dressing

4 slices bacon, cooked and crumbled

3 green onions, thinly sliced

4 oz (113 g) shredded mozzarella cheese

4 oz (113 g) shredded cheddar cheese

16 oz (454 g) pizza dough, at room temperature

¼ cup (45 g) grated Parmesan cheese

Preheat the oven to 425°F (218°C).

Combine the chicken, ranch, bacon, green onions, mozzarella and cheddar cheese in a small bowl. Then, set aside.

Roll out the pizza dough and cut into eight equal squares. Mine kind of resembled squares . . . they don't have to be perfect!

Lightly spray a muffin tin with nonstick cooking spray and press a dough square into each well, so it covers the sides and bottom.

Equally distribute the chicken mixture among the dough cups and sprinkle the tops with the Parmesan.

Bake for 10 to 15 minutes, or until the cheese is bubbling and the crust is golden brown. Twist the pizza cups out of the muffin tin and allow to cool for just a minute or so before serving.

MEDITERRANEAN CHICKEN PITA TACOS

YIELD: 4 SERVINGS

This recipe is a delicious twist on Taco Tuesday! We have tacos almost every Tuesday, and it's great because my family seriously cannot get enough of them. I like to put a fun spin on it every now and then and stray away from traditional tacos. These Mediterranean tacos are the perfect way to do just that.

½ cup (118 ml) plain Greek yogurt

1 tbsp (15 ml) fresh lemon juice

½ tsp dried basil

½ tsp dried oregano

½ tsp salt

¼ tsp fresh ground black pepper

½ tsp dried rosemary

2 rotisserie chicken breasts, diced

½ English cucumber, seeded and diced

1 Roma tomato, chopped

¼ red onion, diced

3 oz (85 g) feta cheese

¼ cup (10 g) chopped fresh cilantro

¼ cup (59 ml) red wine vinaigrette

4 pitas

Combine the Greek yogurt, lemon juice, basil, oregano, salt, pepper and rosemary in a small bowl and set aside.

Combine the chicken, cucumber, tomato, onion, feta cheese and cilantro in a medium bowl. Toss with the vinaigrette.

Fill the pitas with the chicken mixture and drizzle the Greek yogurt sauce on the top.

NOTE: Some pitas will need to be warmed before folding.

BAKED CHIPOTLE CHICKEN AND BLACK BEAN FLAUTAS

YIELD: 8 FLAUTAS

If you've ever wondered what the difference between a taquito and a flauta is, the answer is simple: Taquitos are made with corn tortillas, while flautas are made with flour tortillas. This recipe is so hearty and delicious that it's always a hit with my husband and kids. Chipotle peppers are definitely on the spicy side, so adjust the amount according to your family's preference.

I chose to bake these flautas because 1) it's a healthier choice and 2) everyone gets to eat hot flautas at the same time. When you fry flautas, they have to be done in batches—meaning Mommy gets to hear the moans and groans of delight while she stands over hot oil flipping more flautas. Not cool. This recipe lets everyone enjoy dinner together, and that, my friends, is always the BEST kind of meal.

1 cup (125 g) shredded rotisserie chicken, I like a combination of dark and white

1 cup (227 g) black beans, rinsed and drained

1 chipotle pepper, finely diced

2 tbsp (30 ml) adobo sauce

8 soft taco flour tortillas

8 oz (227 g) grated pepper jack cheese, if that's too spicy go with a Mexican blend instead

Cooking spray or olive oil

OPTIONAL TOPPINGS

Salsa

Sour cream

Guacamole

Preheat the oven to 425°F (218°C).

Combine the shredded chicken, black beans, diced chipotle and adobo sauce in a small bowl. Be careful, the chipotles are spicy! Make sure to wash your hands after working with them.

Spray a large baking sheet with nonstick cooking spray and set aside.

Spoon about ¼ cup (30 g) of the chicken mixture onto a tortilla and top with 2 tablespoons (15 g) of cheese. Roll the tortilla up tightly and place, seam side down, on the prepared baking sheet. Continue assembling the flautas, one at a time, until you're done.

Once all of the flautas have been assembled, spray their tops with additional cooking spray or brush lightly with olive oil. Bake for 10 minutes, flip each one over and bake for 5 additional minutes. They should be a nice golden brown.

We enjoy our flautas with salsa, sour cream and guacamole. Fiesta time!

CHEESY CHICKEN BAKES

YIELD: 4 SERVINGS

There is a certain big-box store that sells these outrageous chicken bakes that my family can't get enough of. Good news? You can easily make them at home.

Caesar dressing, chicken, bacon and loads of cheese are baked inside a Parmesan-coated crust for the ultimate handheld comfort food.

16 oz (454 g) pizza dough, at room temperature

2 cups (250 g) diced rotisserie chicken, white meat only

½ cup (118 ml) refrigerated Caesar dressing

1 oz (28 g) grated Parmesan cheese

8 oz (227 g) shredded mozzarella cheese

3 green onions, thinly sliced

6 slices bacon, cooked and crumbled

1 egg, lightly beaten

Parmesan cheese, to sprinkle on the dough

Preheat the oven to 500°F (260°C). Preheat a pizza stone or line a baking sheet with parchment paper.

Cut the pizza dough into four equal pieces, or as close to equal as you can get.

Roll out each piece into a rectangle about 9" x 5" (23 x 13 cm) and let the dough rest for a few minutes.

Combine the chicken, Caesar dressing, cheeses, green onions and bacon in a medium bowl and toss to combine. You want to make sure that everything is nicely coated with the dressing. Then, set aside.

Roll out the dough again if necessary.

Divide the filling equally among the four sections of dough, placing it on the center of each rectangle. Make sure to leave 1" to 2" (2.5 to 5 cm) of border clear. Brush the beaten egg on the border and then fold the short sides in, just like you would a burrito.

Brush the beaten egg on the newly exposed edges, and then grab one long edge and fold over the filling. Continue rolling until you finish with the seam side down. Brush the tops with more egg wash and sprinkle with additional Parmesan cheese.

Carefully transfer each bake to the preheated pizza stone or prepared baking sheet. Bake for 10 minutes, or until the top of each bake is golden brown.

Let cool for several minutes before eating.

SPICY SAUSAGE AND CHICKEN STROMBOLI

YIELD: 2 STROMBOLI OR 8 SERVINGS

If you've never had stromboli, prepare your taste buds for a new and exciting taste adventure! Stromboli is like pizza, but better. This version has both sausage and chicken, and trust me, this is a good call.

This recipe makes two stromboli using store-bought pizza dough. It's perfect for dinner or game day and is best served with a crisp, green salad.

12 oz (340 g) spicy Italian sausage

1 ½ cups (190 g) diced rotisserie chicken

16 oz (454 g) pizza dough, at room temperature

2 tsp (2 g) Italian seasoning

¼ cup (59 ml) pizza sauce

8 oz (227 g) shredded mozzarella cheese

1 oz (28 g) grated Parmesan cheese

1 egg, lightly beaten

Preheat the oven to 500°F (260°C).

Brown the sausage in a sauté pan over medium-high heat. Stir in the chicken, making sure to coat it with the drippings from the sausage. Remove from the heat and set aside.

Cut the pizza dough into two equal pieces and roll each one into a rectangle roughly 14" x 10" (36 x 25 cm).

Sprinkle about half of the Italian seasoning and spread half of the pizza sauce on each rectangle. Next, sprinkle about ¼ cup (45 g) of the mozzarella cheese on the center of each rectangle, leaving a 2-inch (5-cm) border clear. Equally divide the sausage and chicken mixture among the two rectangles and sprinkle the remaining mozzarella and the Parmesan on top.

Brush the exposed edges with the beaten egg. Fold the two short ends in and brush the newly exposed dough with the egg wash. Roll up the stromboli like you would a burrito, making sure to end with the seam side down.

Carefully transfer each stromboli to a baking sheet or pizza stone and bake for 10 to 12 minutes, or until golden brown. Let the stromboli cool for several minutes before placing on a cutting board to slice it. Serve immediately.

MEDITERRANEAN CHICKEN PINWHEELS

YIELD: 4 SERVINGS

There was a three- to four-month period in my life where I made wraps for lunch every single day. Not the same kind of course, but the process was always the same. I would spread a flavored cream cheese on a tortilla, top it with some sort of meat and finish it off with spinach or lettuce. I was addicted.

This recipe is just an idea of what you can do with your wraps at home. Feel free to substitute, alter or totally change any or all of the ingredients to suit your liking. I have to say, though, that this Mediterranean version is the bomb dot com. Quick, easy, delicious.

8 oz (227 g) cream cheese, softened

4 artichoke hearts, drained and diced

4 strips roasted red pepper, diced

A handful of sliced black olives, diced

1 rotisserie chicken breast, diced

4 flatbreads or wraps, I used Lavash

Baby spinach

Combine all of the ingredients, except for the flatbread and spinach, in the bowl of a mixer. Turn the mixer on low and let 'er rip. You want all those flavors to mingle and marry.

Spread a thin layer of the chicken and cream cheese mixture on top of your flatbread or wrap. Top with a single layer of baby spinach leaves. You'll need 15 to 20 leaves depending on the size of your flatbread.

Roll tightly and slice into six to eight pinwheels. Repeat the process with the remaining flatbreads, filling and spinach.

NOTE: Most artichokes come packed in water, either in a jar or can. Make sure to actually squeeze the artichokes (over your sink) to get rid of all that excess liquid before dicing and adding them to the mixer.

ROASTED VEGGIE PESTO TART

YIELD: 6 SERVINGS

Bring on the veggies! I grow lots of fresh vegetables during the summer months, and this pesto tart is one of my favorite ways to use the squash that keeps cropping up overnight. Paired with a delightful puff pastry crust and *herbalicious* pesto—this tart is the perfect summer fare! All those veggies plus juicy, flavorful rotisserie chicken turn this tart into a filling and delicious dinner!

1 zucchini, thinly sliced

1 yellow squash, thinly sliced

2 tbsp (30 ml) olive oil

Salt and pepper, to taste

1 (17 ⅓ oz [490 g]) package puff pastry, thawed

1 ½ cups (190 g) diced rotisserie chicken

7 oz (198 g) pesto

½ pint (193 g) cherry or grape tomatoes, halved (if large)

8 oz (227 g) fresh mozzarella, thinly sliced

Preheat the oven to 450°F (232°C).

Place the zucchini and squash in a single layer on a large baking sheet. Drizzle the veggies with the olive oil and sprinkle with salt and pepper to taste. Roast in the oven for 10 minutes. Remove the zucchini and squash and place on paper towels to soak up any excess moisture.

Reduce the oven temperature to 425°F (218°C).

On a lightly floured cutting board, roll out each puff pastry sheet to a 10" x 14" (25 x 36 cm) rectangle and transfer to two 15" x 10" (38 x 25 cm) jelly roll pans lined with parchment paper. Poke each puff pastry sheet all over with a fork and bake for 10 minutes. The pastry will puff up during baking, so simply press it down in the center with a spatula. Then, set aside.

Toss the chicken with about half of the pesto and spread the other half of pesto on top of each puff pastry. Top with the tomatoes, chicken, zucchini, squash and cheese. Return the tarts to the oven and bake for another 10 to 12 minutes, or until the cheese has melted and the pastry is nice and golden.

Cut into squares and serve.

NAVAJO TACOS

YIELD: 10 TACOS

Your family is in for a real treat when you make these Navajo Tacos for dinner! I like to serve these as a taco bar, so everyone can put their favorite fixings on their tacos. It's fun for the family and it's also less work for me—a win-win!

½ cup (85 g) yellow cornmeal

4 to 5 cups (500 to 625 g) all-purpose flour

½ tsp salt

2 tsp (8 g) baking powder

1 ½ cups (355 ml) water

½ cup (118 ml) milk

Vegetable oil, for frying

2 cups (250 g) shredded rotisserie chicken

½ cup (118 ml) salsa

1 (16 oz [454 g]) can refried beans

8 oz (227 g) shredded Mexican blend cheese

Shredded lettuce

Diced tomatoes

Sour cream

Combine the cornmeal, 4 cups (500 g) of flour, salt and baking powder in a large bowl. Stir in the water and milk and knead for 2 to 3 minutes, adding more flour as necessary to keep the dough from sticking too much.

Heat the oil in a large, deep skillet to 375°F (191°C). Make sure the oil is at least 1 inch (2.5 cm) deep.

Divide the dough into 10 balls and press each one into rough circles on a lightly floured surface. Rustic is better here, so don't be fussy. Make a small hole in the center of each circle with your finger—this helps the frying process. Carefully place the dough into the oil, putting the side closest to you in first (this keeps the oil from splashing on you). I can usually fit two or three in the skillet at the same time.

Fry for about 2 minutes on each side, or until it puffs and turns golden brown. Poke any bubbles that form with a wooden spoon. Remove the fried dough and drain on paper towels.

Combine the chicken and salsa in a microwave-safe bowl and heat on high in 30-second increments, stirring in between, until warm.

Time to top these babies! Start by spreading on a thin layer of refried beans, and then add the chicken mixture, cheese, lettuce, tomatoes, sour cream and anything else you want. Kids LOVE these tacos!

NOTE: Make a double batch of these shells and douse them with powdered sugar and honey for a quick and tasty dessert!

MEXICAN PIZZAS

YIELD: 4 PIZZAS

You've probably noticed that I have a lot of Mexican recipes in this book. I can't help it. We eat A LOT of Mexican food around here. When you combine the words "Mexican" and "pizza" in our home, it's cause for celebration. Two worlds colliding and exploding into a flavor riot in your mouth. Make your tummy happy tonight!

1 (16 oz [454 g]) can refried beans, you may not need the entire can

2 cups (250 g) shredded rotisserie chicken

½ cup (118 ml) salsa

Vegetable oil, for frying

8 flour tortillas, fajita or taco size

1 (10 oz [283 g]) can enchilada sauce, you will need only about half a can

8 oz (227 g) shredded Mexican blend cheese

2 green onions, thinly sliced

2 Roma tomatoes, diced

Preheat the oven to 350°F (177°C).

Warm up the refried beans in the microwave or a small saucepan. Combine the chicken and salsa in a small bowl and stir to combine. Warm up the mixture in the microwave or a small saucepan. Then, set aside.

Heat the oil to 350°F (177°C) in a large skillet. You don't need the oil to be very deep since you will be flipping the tortillas. Fry each tortilla for 1 to 2 minutes per side, or just until golden brown. Use tongs to poke down any bubbles that pop up while you are frying.

Lay the tortillas on a flat surface. Spread about 2 tablespoons (30 g) of the refried beans on four of the fried tortillas. Top with the chicken mixture, evenly dividing it among the four tortillas. Top each tortilla with one of the remaining tortillas.

Spread a thin layer of enchilada sauce on the top of each tortilla and sprinkle with the shredded cheese, evenly dividing it among the four pizzas. Move the pizzas to a baking sheet and bake for 5 to 7 minutes, or until the cheese has completely melted.

Top with the green onions and diced tomatoes. *Delicioso!*

CHICKEN TACO CUPS

YIELD: 8 TACO CUPS

We have tacos for dinner a couple of times a month. I mean, it just doesn't get any easier than tacos for dinner. Every now and then, I like to liven up dinnertime with these fun taco cups. You can fill them with whatever you want, and that's half the fun!

8 flour tortillas, fajita size OR the smallest size you can find

2 cups (250 g) shredded rotisserie chicken

½ cup (118 ml) salsa

1 (16 oz [454 g]) can refried beans, you may not need the entire can

4 oz (113 g) shredded Mexican blend cheese

TOPPINGS

Sour cream

Black olives

Sliced green onions

Cilantro

Diced tomatoes

Salsa

Shredded lettuce

Guacamole

Preheat the oven to 350°F (177°C).

Spray a muffin tin with nonstick cooking spray. Gently press the tortillas into the wells and spray the tops with cooking spray. Bake for 10 minutes.

While the taco cups are baking, combine the chicken and salsa in a small bowl.

Remove the taco cups from the oven and fill with refried beans, the chicken mixture and shredded cheese. Return the muffin tin to the oven and bake for 5 more minutes, or until the cheese has melted.

Top with your choice of toppings.

CHAPTER 5

SLOW COOKER CREATIONS

I'm not ashamed to admit that I own seven—SEVEN!—slow cookers. I'm a teensy bit addicted. I've been known to have three or more slow cookers bubbling away at the same time. What can I say? I'm nothing if not efficient.

Slow cookers are the perfect way to save your sanity and time in the kitchen. They are the epitome of the "set it and forget it" meal, and there is just NOTHING better than coming home to a hot meal that's ready to go.

I love a good variety when it comes to slow cooker recipes, and I hope you do too. Make sure to check out the Chicken and Spinach Lasagna Rolls (page 114), the Chicken Chile Verde (page 116) and the Chicken Cacciatore (page 119)—some of our favorites!

CHICKEN PHILLY CHEESESTEAKS

YIELD: 6 SANDWICHES

These cheesesteaks are so not traditional, but they should be! I have a steak version on my blog that is super popular and gets great reviews, but I knew I wanted to make a chicken version for this book. Like all slow cooker meals, this recipe is great at taking the stress out of dinnertime. This is a truly delicious meal that is so easy to make any night of the week!

3 cups (375 g) sliced rotisserie chicken

½ tsp fresh ground black pepper

1 tsp garlic powder

1 medium onion, thinly sliced

1 bell pepper, sliced

32 oz (907 ml) low-sodium chicken broth

6 French rolls

12 slices provolone cheese

Combine all ingredients, except for the rolls and cheese, in the slow cooker. Cook on low for 5 to 7 hours, or until you get home from soccer practice. You can't overcook the chicken—it just gets more and more tender.

Throw the rolls in a 400°F (205°C) oven for 3 to 5 minutes, or until slightly crusty. This keeps them from getting soggy later on.

Lay a piece of provolone cheese on each side of the rolls. Use tongs to remove the chicken, onion and bell pepper from the slow cooker and pile on top of the rolls. Make sure to let the excess juices drip off first.

Return the sandwiches to the oven for another 3 to 5 minutes to melt the cheese. Serve with sweet potato fries and a salad.

NOTE: Pick up one kind of bell pepper or go crazy like I do and pick up one red, orange, yellow and green and turn these cheesesteaks into Rainbow Chicken Cheesesteaks!

SALSA CHICKEN QUINOA CASSEROLE

YIELD: 6 SERVINGS

If you haven't tried quinoa before, let this delicious and easy recipe be your first time. This hearty and healthy casserole is a great introduction to quinoa and one your whole family will love. The cheesy topping itself is delicious, and the casserole is just LOADED with amazing Mexican flavors. Get ready to dive in!

2 cups (250 g) shredded rotisserie chicken

8 oz (227 g) rainbow quinoa, or any other quinoa

1 (15 oz [425 g]) can black beans, rinsed and drained

1 (15 ¼ oz [432 g]) can sweet corn, drained

2 cups (438 ml) salsa, use your favorite brand

2 cups (480 ml) low-sodium chicken broth, divided

8 oz (227 g) shredded Mexican blend cheese OR Monterey Jack cheese, divided

1 (4 oz [113 g]) can diced green chiles, not drained

5 oz (142 g) queso fresco, crumbled

1 tsp ground cumin

½ tsp salt

½ tsp fresh ground black pepper

OPTIONAL TOPPINGS

Cilantro

Tomatoes

Avocado

Green onion

Olives

Salsa

Combine all of the ingredients—except 4 ounces (113 g) of the Monterey Jack cheese and 1 cup (240 ml) of the broth—in a 4- to 5-quart (4- to 5-L) slow cooker. Smooth out the top.

Add the remaining broth and Monterey Jack cheese over the ingredients. Place the lid and cook on low for 6 to 8 hours, or until the quinoa is fully cooked.

Serve with your choice of toppings: cilantro, tomatoes, avocado, green onion, olives or salsa.

NOTE: Rinse the beans until there are no more bubbles. No bubbles on the beans, no bubbles in you later.

SAUSAGE AND CHICKEN STUFFED PEPPERS

YIELD: 8 SERVINGS

A few years ago, I made stuffed peppers for the first time at the request of my husband. We loved them!

This recipe is a variation on those peppers, and it's made in the slow cooker. It's the most amazing dinner to come home to because the flavors are so fresh and vibrant.

1 cup (211 g) rice, uncooked

8 bell peppers, various colors

2 tbsp (30 ml) olive oil

1 medium onion, diced

3 cloves garlic, minced

½ tsp salt

½ tsp fresh ground black pepper

6 oz (170 g) andouille sausage OR kielbasa OR another type cooked sausage, chopped

2 cups (250 g) diced rotisserie chicken

1 (10 oz [283 g]) can diced tomatoes and green chilies

8 oz (227 g) pepper jack cheese, grated, divided

Cook the rice according to package directions. You can either use water or reduced-sodium chicken broth for the cooking liquid.

Cut the tops off the bell peppers (where the stems are located) and use a spoon to remove as much as possible of the seeds and veins. Don't throw away the tops! Dice the usable parts of the bell pepper tops and set aside.

Heat the olive oil in a large sauté pan over medium-high heat. Add the diced bell pepper tops and onion and cook, stirring occasionally, until the onion is soft and translucent, about 6 to 8 minutes.

Stir in the minced garlic and continue cooking for an additional minute. Season with the salt and pepper. Stir in the sausage and chicken and cook for another 2 to 3 minutes.

Combine the pepper and meat mixture with the rice and stir to combine. Add the canned diced tomatoes and chilies and about ⅔ (5 oz [151 g]) of the grated cheese to the mixture.

Spoon the filling into the empty bell peppers and place them in the slow cooker. Replace the lid and cook on low for 6 to 8 hours, or until the peppers are nice and tender.

Sprinkle the remaining cheese on top of the peppers about 30 minutes before they are done, replace the lid and finish cooking. Enjoy!

NOTE: Choose a variety of peppers for an impressive presentation. If you can't find orange or yellow bell peppers, feel free to substitute the red and green varieties, which are easier to find.

SLOW COOKER CHICKEN AND SPINACH LASAGNA ROLLS

YIELD: 6 SERVINGS

I don't think a week goes by that I don't crave lasagna in some form or another, but these rolls are always fun to make—especially in the slow cooker! The lasagna noodles are rolled up with a spinach, chicken, herb and ricotta filling and slow cooked, resulting in a hearty, cheesy and EASY Italian-style dinner any night of the week.

1 (12 oz [340 g]) package lasagna noodles, you will need about half

1 (24 oz [680 g]) jar marinara sauce, your favorite brand

1 (15 oz [425 g]) container ricotta

1 (10 oz [283 g]) package frozen spinach, thawed and drained

4 oz (113 g) grated Parmesan cheese

8 oz (227 g) shredded mozzarella cheese

2 eggs, lightly beaten

2 cups (250 g) diced rotisserie chicken

1 tbsp (3 g) chopped fresh thyme

1 tbsp (3 g) chopped fresh oregano

½ tsp salt

½ tsp fresh ground black pepper

4 oz (113 g) shredded mozzarella, optional

Cook about half of the lasagna noodles according to the package instructions. You will need 10 to 12 noodles.

Pour about half of the jar of marinara into your slow cooker.

Combine the ricotta, spinach, Parmesan, mozzarella, eggs, chicken, thyme, oregano, salt and pepper in a large bowl and mix.

Lay the noodles out on a flat surface and generously spread the ricotta mixture onto each one. Roll up the lasagna noodles and place in the slow cooker. Continue until you have used up all of the filling or all of the noodles. I usually end up with a couple extra noodles. Top with the remaining marinara sauce and cook on low for 6 to 8 hours.

If using the optional 4 ounces (113 g) of mozzarella cheese, remove the lid from the slow cooker and sprinkle the cheese on top of the rolls. Replace the lid and continue cooking for another 10 minutes, or until the cheese has melted.

Serve with Parmesan cheese and a fresh garden salad for an easy Italian dinner.

NOTE: Place a paper towel between the lid and the insert of the slow cooker to collect the steam. Now when you open your lid, a stream of water won't drip on the food below.

*See photo on page 106.

CHICKEN ENCHILADA CASSEROLE

YIELD: 6 SERVINGS

My boys could eat Mexican food three times a day. Enchiladas are their very favorite, and making them in the slow cooker makes them my favorite too. I love a good "set it and forget" it meal, and this one is as good as it gets. All you need to do is spoon the casserole out of the slow cooker and serve it with sour cream, avocados and salsa. Fiesta time!

1 (28 oz [784 g]) can red enchilada sauce, divided

8 oz (227 g) shredded Mexican blend cheese, divided

3 cups (375 g) shredded rotisserie chicken

1 (2 ¼ oz [64 g]) can sliced black olives, drained (optional)

½ cup (120 ml) low-sodium chicken broth

12 yellow corn tortillas

Reserve ½ cup (118 ml) enchilada sauce and 2 ounces (57 g) cheese for the topping.

Combine the chicken, olives (if using), chicken broth, 6 ounces (170 g) of the cheese and ½ cup (118 ml) of the enchilada sauce in a medium bowl. Then, set aside.

Add just enough enchilada sauce to cover the bottom of your slow cooker insert.

Place a few of the tortillas on top of the sauce, tearing to make them fit if necessary. It's okay if they overlap a little bit. Next, spoon on some of the chicken mixture followed by some of the enchilada sauce. Repeat, with layers of tortillas, chicken mixture and enchilada sauce until you run out.

Finish with a layer of tortillas and top with the reserved enchilada sauce and cheese.

Cook on low for 6 to 8 hours.

NOTE: Place a paper towel between the slow cooker insert and the lid to absorb excess moisture.

SLOW COOKER CHICKEN CHILE VERDE

YIELD: 8 SERVINGS

Chile verde simply means "green chile" in Spanish, and that's the base of this mouthwatering recipe. It's a delicious Mexican dish that is traditionally made with pork. Tomatillos are broiled along with a variety of peppers and then blended to a salsa-like consistency. An entire rotisserie chicken and a handful of other ingredients complete the list.

This is a slow cooker recipe that will rock your world with its awesome flavor. Of all the recipes I made for this book, this was my oldest son's favorite. He ate four bowls the first night and was asking for more the next day. I have to say, it feels so good putting all these fresh, gorgeous ingredients together for an incredible meal for my family!

10 tomatillos, husks removed

2 Anaheim peppers

2 poblano peppers

2 serrano peppers

4 tbsp (59 ml) olive oil, divided

2 medium onions, diced

1 jalapeño, diced

3 cloves garlic, minced

½ tsp kosher salt

½ tsp fresh ground black pepper

1 tsp ground cumin

1 tsp dried oregano

1 bunch of cilantro

1 rotisserie chicken, pulled, shredded or cubed

1 cup (240 ml) low-sodium chicken stock

1 (4 oz [113 g]) can diced green chiles

Corn tortillas, warmed, to serve

Preheat the broiler. Rinse the tomatillos and Anaheim, poblano and serrano peppers and pat dry. Place on a large baking sheet and drizzle with about 1 to 2 tablespoons (15 to 30 ml) of olive oil.

Pop under the broiler for about 8 minutes, flipping the peppers over halfway through. You want the tomatillos and peppers to blister and blacken. This is a good thing. Remove the peppers from under the broiler and place in a plastic resealable bag right away. Let the tomatillos rest. Then, set aside.

Heat the remaining 2 tablespoons (30 ml) of olive oil in a medium skillet over medium-high heat. Add the diced onions and jalapeño and sauté, stirring frequently, for 5 to 6 minutes or until the onions are translucent. Stir in the minced garlic, salt, black pepper, cumin and oregano. Continue cooking for another 1 to 2 minutes. Remove from heat.

Back to the peppers that have been steaming away in the bag. . . . Remove the peppers from the bag and use a paper towel to wipe off their skin. It should peel off easily. Remove the stems and the seeds, but don't worry about the stragglers.

Add the tomatillos (whole), peeled peppers and cilantro to a blender and puree for 1 to 2 minutes. Then, set aside.

Time to pull it all together! Transfer the chicken to a 4-quart (4-L) slow cooker. Add in the contents of the blender, the sautéed veggies, chicken broth and the green chiles. Stir gently to combine. Cook on low for 6 to 8 hours. Serve with warm corn tortillas.

NOTE: If you're pressed for time in the morning, feel free to do the broiler and blender portion of the recipe the night before to make things easier. Like it spicy? Add an extra jalapeño!

SLOW COOKER CHICKEN CACCIATORE

YIELD: 6 SERVINGS

Talk about hearty! This slow cooker meal is the perfect way to warm up on a cold night after a long day's work. We go back and forth as to whether chicken cacciatore should be served over rice or pasta, but both ways are delicious. Combine this recipe with a piece of bread slathered with garlic butter and a fresh garden salad for the perfect lazy day dinner.

2 tbsp (30 ml) olive oil

1 bell pepper, diced

1 onion, thinly sliced

8 oz (227 g) sliced white mushrooms

2 cloves garlic, minced

1 tsp salt

½ tsp fresh ground black pepper

2 tsp (2 g) minced fresh oregano

½ tsp minced fresh rosemary

1 tsp minced fresh basil

1 bay leaf

1 (24 oz [680 g]) jar marinara sauce

½ cup (120 ml) red wine

3 cups (460 g) rotisserie chicken pieces, dark meat preferable

Pasta OR rice, cooked according to package directions

Heat the olive oil in a medium sauté pan over medium-high heat. Add the bell pepper, onion and mushrooms. Sauté for 5 to 6 minutes, or until the onion is soft and translucent. Stir in the garlic, salt, black pepper, oregano, rosemary, basil and the bay leaf. Cook for an additional 1 to 2 minutes. Then, set aside.

Add the marinara and red wine to a 4-quart (4-L) slow cooker. Add the chicken and sautéed vegetables. Stir to combine. Cook on low for 6 to 8 hours. Remove the bay leaf and discard.

Serve over cooked pasta or rice. Garnish with sprigs of rosemary and oregano, if desired.

NOTE: I like to use the dark meat from the rotisserie chicken for this recipe as it really adds to the richness of the dish. I just pull off all the dark meat that I can and supplement with white meat if necessary.

SLOW COOKER CHICKEN MINESTRONE

YIELD: 8 SERVINGS

Credit for this recipe idea goes to my husband. We were at our favorite local Italian restaurant for dinner, and he ordered his usual, minestrone soup. As I watched him slurp down all those delicious vegetables, he looked up at me and said, "You should make a chicken minestrone soup for your book!" So I did. And he was right.

When cooking veggies in the slow cooker, I find that sautéing them first really brings out their flavors. It's a small step that has a big payoff for sure.

2 tbsp (30 ml) olive oil

2 tbsp (29 g) unsalted butter

2 stalks celery, sliced

2 carrots, diced

8 oz (227 g) sliced mushrooms

1 onion, diced

2 cloves garlic, minced

2 tbsp (3 g) dried parsley

1 tsp dried oregano

1 tsp dried basil

1 tsp salt

1 tsp fresh ground black pepper

1 (28 oz [794 g]) can crushed tomatoes

1 (14 ½ oz [411 g]) can diced tomatoes

2 cups (480 ml) low-sodium chicken broth

8 oz (227 g) fresh green beans, cut into 1" (2.5 cm) pieces

1 (15 oz [425 g]) can great northern OR cannellini beans, rinsed and drained

2 cups (250 g) shredded rotisserie chicken

12 oz (340 g) ditalini or macaroni pasta, cooked according to package directions

Parmesan cheese, to serve

Heat the olive oil and butter in a medium sauté pan over medium-high heat. Add the celery, carrots, mushrooms and onion and sauté for 5 to 6 minutes, or until the onion is soft and translucent.

Stir in the garlic, parsley, oregano, basil, salt and pepper and cook for an additional 1 to 2 minutes, stirring frequently.

Add the crushed and diced tomatoes to the slow cooker alongside the sautéed veggies. Stir in the chicken broth, green beans and canned beans.

Cook on low for 6 to 8 hours. Stir in the shredded chicken and pasta and cook on low for another 15 to 30 minutes, or until the chicken is heated through.

Serve with Parmesan cheese.

NOTE: Rinse the beans until no more bubbles appear. Trust me on this.

SLOW COOKER PULLED BARBECUE CHICKEN SLIDERS

YIELD: 4 SERVINGS

The pulling of the chicken happens first, instead of last, in this pulled chicken recipe. It's kind of nice not to burn my fingers for once. . . . Make sure you use your favorite barbecue sauce here because the flavors really intensify in the slow cooker. The chicken gets so tender, saucy and delicious while it cooks.

I used pretzel slider buns. Not only are they super cute, they also taste fantastic with the pulled barbecue chicken. I love coleslaw on my hot sandwiches, but if you're not a fan, feel free to eliminate it from this recipe.

These sliders are super quick and easy, plus they're the perfect size for little hands yet hearty enough for big appetites.

1 tbsp (15 ml) olive oil

½ onion, thinly sliced

¼ tsp salt

¼ tsp fresh ground black pepper

2 cups (250 g) shredded rotisserie chicken

¾ cup (177 ml) barbecue sauce

¼ cup (59 ml) low-sodium chicken broth

8 slider buns

8 slices sharp cheddar cheese

Coleslaw (optional)

Heat the olive oil in a small sauté pan over medium heat. Add the onion and sauté for 4 to 5 minutes, or until the onion is translucent. Season with the salt and pepper.

Transfer the onion, chicken, barbecue sauce and chicken broth to a 2-quart (2-L) slow cooker and stir to combine. Cook on low for 3 to 5 hours.

Divide the chicken mixture evenly among the buns. Top with the cheese and coleslaw, if desired. Serve immediately.

SLOW COOKER CHICKEN BROTH

YIELD: 5 PINTS (2.4 L)

If there's one slow cooker recipe that is absolutely essential, it's this one. I would say close to one quarter of the recipes in this book call for chicken broth. Now, of course you can use store-bought chicken broth or stock, but why not make your own?

After you've pulled all the meat off of your chicken, use that carcass to make some of the most delicious chicken broth ever, right in your slow cooker!

1 rotisserie chicken carcass

2 carrots, rinsed and cut into 2" (5 cm) pieces

2 stalks celery, rinsed and cut into 2" (5 cm) pieces

1 onion, quartered

1 bay leaf

1 tsp salt

½ tsp fresh ground black pepper

10 to 12 cups (2.4 to 2.8 L) water

Pick the chicken carcass clean, removing as much of the skin and meat as possible, and place it in a 6-quart (6-L) slow cooker. Add the carrots, celery, onion, bay leaf, salt and pepper. Add just enough water to cover the chicken completely.

Set your slow cooker to low and cook for 8 to 10 hours, or overnight.

Pour the contents of the slow cooker through a fine mesh sieve. Discard everything but the broth.

Pour the broth into jars and refrigerate for up to 4 days, or transfer the broth to freezer-safe containers and freeze for up to 3 months. If storing the broth in bags, freeze them on a flat surface so they can be stored more easily in your freezer.

To defrost the broth, place the frozen broth in your refrigerator and let thaw overnight.

NOTE: You can also add herbs to your slow cooker if you'd like. Parsley, oregano and thyme all work beautifully. Just make sure that you label your broth before freezing so you know what herbs have been added.

CHAPTER 6

COMFORT FOODS

Ahh, my favorite type of food! This is the chapter you'll want to turn to when you're looking for food that warms the soul. Whether we're talking pizza, spaghetti or enchiladas—this chapter has something for everyone. Make sure to check out my favorites: French Spaghetti (page 129), Spinach Artichoke French Bread Pizza (page 137) and Cheesy Chicken Tamales (page 144)!

FRENCH SPAGHETTI

YIELD: 6 SERVINGS

Welcome to your new favorite spaghetti recipe! This recipe is a family heirloom. I'll admit that I was a little nervous trying to revamp such a treasured recipe, but the results were more than spectacular. The original recipe calls for braising chicken thighs for hours—HOURS. Who has time for that? I am loving this version with the rotisserie chicken—so easy, and I don't have to pick out any bones.

Regarding this recipe, my mom always said, if it looks like it needs a little more wine, go for it! So feel free to add as needed.

2 tbsp (30 ml) extra virgin olive oil

¼ cup (57 g) butter

1 large onion, diced

2 cloves garlic, minced

¼ tsp dried rosemary

⅛ tsp dried oregano

⅛ tsp dried thyme

1 tbsp (2 g) dried parsley

1 (29 oz [822 g]) can tomato sauce

½ cup (120 ml) burgundy wine

2 bay leaves

1 (1 ½ oz [43 g]) package spaghetti sauce seasoning

3 cups (375 g) shredded rotisserie chicken

16 oz (454 g) thin spaghetti, cooked

Parmesan cheese, to serve

Drizzle the olive oil in a 4-quart (4-L) heavy-bottomed pot over medium-high heat. Melt the butter and add the diced onion. Sauté for about 4 to 5 minutes, or until the onion is soft and translucent.

Stir in the minced garlic and cook for another minute, stirring frequently. We do NOT want that garlic to burn!

Stir in the herbs. Add the tomato sauce and wine and stir to combine. Finally, stir in the bay leaves, spaghetti sauce seasoning and shredded chicken.

Bring to a simmer and cook for at least 20 minutes, stirring frequently.

Now, when my grandma makes this dish, she adds the pasta to the spaghetti sauce right in the pot. It's then transferred to a GIANT serving dish and topped with liberal amounts of Parmesan cheese. It's outright fabulous. Do as my grandma did, or top the cooked spaghetti with the sauce and then douse it with Parmesan cheese. You'll be in heaven either way.

GREEN CHILE AND CREAM CHEESE ENCHILADAS

YIELD: 5 SERVINGS OR 10 ENCHILADAS

Enchiladas the way my Nana used to make them! My Nana knew a secret that I'm going to share with you now: Cream cheese makes everything better! These enchiladas are so creamy and delicious, and I encourage you to go nuts with the toppings: cilantro, avocados, tomatoes, green onions and sour cream—use it all!

You'll notice that I use flour tortillas for these enchiladas. I'm lazy. I find the flour tortillas are pliable enough that they don't require warming as do corn tortillas. If you want to use corn tortillas, go for it! Just don't forget the cream cheese.

28 oz (793 g) green enchilada sauce, divided

2 ½ cups (315 g) shredded rotisserie chicken

8 oz (227 g) cream cheese, softened

1 (4 oz [113 g]) can diced green chiles

8 oz (227 g) shredded Monterey Jack cheese, divided

10 flour tortillas, burrito size

Preheat the oven to 350°F (177°C).

Lightly spray a 9" x 13" (23 x 33 cm) baking dish with nonstick cooking spray. Add about half of the enchilada sauce to the bottom of the baking dish.

Combine the chicken, cream cheese, chiles and 6 ounces (170 g) of the Monterey Jack cheese in a medium bowl and mix well.

Spoon about ½ cup (121 g) of the filling onto the center of a tortilla. Roll up tightly and place in the baking dish. Repeat until the filling and all tortillas have been used.

Sprinkle the remaining cheese evenly on the top of the enchiladas. Cover the baking dish with foil and bake for 20 minutes. Remove the foil and return to the oven. Bake for an additional 10 minutes, or until the cheese is melted and bubbling.

Bring out the toppings and enjoy!

COCONUT CURRY CHICKEN

YIELD: 6 SERVINGS

I am a sucker for curry chicken. All those outrageously complex flavors together make me weak in the knees. The coconut milk adds a creaminess and richness to the dish that I adore. Rotisserie chicken makes this dish relatively simple and even more delicious.

1 tbsp (15 ml) vegetable oil

3 tbsp (22 g) curry powder

½ onion, thinly sliced

3 cloves garlic, crushed

½ tsp salt

½ tsp fresh ground black pepper

½ tsp paprika

2 cups (250 g) diced rotisserie chicken

1 (14 ½ oz [411 g]) can stewed tomatoes, do not drain

1 (13 ½ oz [398 ml]) can light coconut milk

2 tbsp (25 g) brown sugar

1 tsp fresh grated ginger

Juice from ½ lime

½ cup (38 g) shredded coconut

¼ cup (28 g) crushed cashews

Cooked rice

2 green onions, thinly sliced

Heat the oil in a large skillet over medium-high heat. Stir in the curry powder and cook, stirring frequently, for 5 to 6 minutes. Add the sliced onion and continue cooking, stirring occasionally, until the onion is translucent, about 4 to 5 minutes. Add the garlic, salt, pepper and paprika and cook for another minute or so, stirring frequently.

Add the chicken and stir to coat. You want all those flavors to start soaking into the chicken.

Add the can of stewed tomatoes, coconut milk, brown sugar and ginger. Stir to combine and bring to a simmer. Simmer, uncovered, for about 40 minutes, stirring occasionally, or until the curry has thickened to your liking. Stir in the lime juice, shredded coconut and cashews.

Serve over cooked rice. Garnish with green onions and additional coconut and cashews, if desired.

MEXICAN MANICOTTI

YIELD: 6 SERVINGS

Our favorite type of cuisine is Mexican. Hands down. We eat it at least twice a week. Sometimes we pretend we're eating some other type of cuisine, but it really has Mexican flavors—much like this manicotti dish where Mexican meets Italian!

1 (8 oz [227 g]) package manicotti

1 (29 oz [822 g]) can tomato sauce

1 (4 oz [113 g]) can diced green chiles

¼ cups (61 g) adobo sauce from a can of chipotle peppers

½ onion, diced

1 tbsp (15 ml) olive oil

1 ½ cups (190 g) minced rotisserie chicken

2 tsp (5 g) taco seasoning

¼ cup (59 ml) water

15 oz (425 g) part-skim ricotta cheese

8 oz (227 g) shredded Mexican blend cheese, divided

Sour cream, for serving

Cilantro, for garnish

Preheat oven to 350°F (177°C). Lightly spray a 9″ x 13″ (23 x 33 cm) baking dish with nonstick cooking spray and set aside.

Cook the manicotti according to the package directions, removing it about 2 minutes shy of al dente. Drain and set aside. Don't worry, the manicotti will finish cooking in the oven.

In a medium bowl, combine the tomato sauce, green chiles and adobo sauce. Pour half of the sauce mixture onto the bottom of the baking dish.

In a medium skillet over medium heat, sauté the onion in the olive oil until translucent, about 4 to 5 minutes. Add the chicken, taco seasoning and water to the skillet. Bring to a simmer and cook for 2 to 3 minutes, or until the water has evaporated.

Combine the chicken mixture, ricotta and 1 cup (121 g) of the shredded cheese in a large bowl. Transfer this mixture to a large resealable bag and cut off one corner, so that you can fit the corner of the bag into the opening of the manicotti. Squeeze gently to fill the manicotti, working from both sides of the manicotti if necessary. Continue until all manicotti have been filled, placing them in the prepared baking dish as you go.

Top the manicotti with the remaining tomato sauce mixture and sprinkle on the remaining shredded cheese. Cover with foil and bake for 30 minutes. Remove the foil and continue baking for an additional 15 minutes, or until the cheese is melted and bubbling. Serve with sour cream and garnish with fresh cilantro.

NOTE: If you want to turn up the heat in this dish, add a diced chipotle pepper to the tomato sauce mixture.

SPINACH ARTICHOKE FRENCH BREAD PIZZA

YIELD: 6 SERVINGS

I took my mom's famous appetizer artichoke dip and turned it into a meal! Adding rotisserie chicken to the mix adds a ton of flavor and heartiness that I love. Artichoke dip has long been a family favorite, and now this pizza is as well. Perfect for busy nights, this recipe is all about the "dump-and-go" method. All of the ingredients are dumped into a bowl and then spread onto French bread—it couldn't be easier!

1 (14 oz [400 g]) can quartered artichoke hearts, packed in water

10 oz (283 g) frozen chopped spinach, thawed and squeezed dry

4 oz (113 g) can diced green chiles

2 cups (250 g) shredded rotisserie chicken, both the white and dark meats are good here

2 oz (57 g) grated Parmesan cheese

4 oz (113 g) shredded Monterey Jack cheese

4 oz (113 g) shredded sharp cheddar cheese

½ cup (118 ml) mayonnaise

2 cloves garlic, minced

1 loaf French bread

Preheat the oven to 350°F (177°C).

Drain the artichokes and roughly chop. Combine with the rest of the ingredients, except for the bread, in a large bowl. Then, set aside.

Carefully cut the loaf of French bread down the center lengthwise. You can scoop out some of the insides or leave it as is. Divide the filling evenly between the two halves and carefully spread it onto each half.

Place the pizzas on a baking sheet and bake for 25 to 30 minutes, or until the cheese has melted and the tops are starting to turn golden brown.

Cut into slices and serve.

CHICKEN MARGHERITA PIZZA

YIELD: 6 SERVINGS OR 2 PIZZAS

I'm not sure there is a better combination of ingredients than that of tomatoes, mozzarella and basil. When they are all fresh and put on a pizza, it's pure bliss! And then, I added rotisserie chicken to this pizza . . . *mind blown*. I think you'll find that chicken most definitely belongs here.

The next time the kids are asking for pizza for dinner, give this one a try!

16 oz (448 g) refrigerated pizza dough, at room temperature, divided

Olive oil

¼ cup (60 ml) pizza sauce, divided

1 rotisserie chicken breast, thinly sliced, divided

8 oz (226 g) fresh mozzarella, sliced, divided

16 oz (454 g) fresh tomatoes, sliced, divided

Fresh basil

Salt and pepper, to taste

Preheat the oven to 500°F (260°C). Place a pizza pan or stone in the oven while it's preheating.

Divide the dough into two pieces and set one aside. Working with one half of the dough, stretch it to fit your pizza pan.

When the oven is preheated, remove the pizza pan or stone, drizzle with olive oil and carefully lay the pizza dough on top. Spoon half of the pizza sauce onto the center of the dough and use the back of a spoon to spread it out. Layer half of the chicken, mozzarella and tomatoes on top, slightly overlapping as you go. Tear up some fresh basil and sprinkle on top. A few leaves is plenty.

Sprinkle on some salt and pepper and drizzle with olive oil. Place the pizza in the oven and cook for 15 to 18 minutes, or until the crust is golden and the cheese is melted. Remove and place on a cutting board and repeat with the remaining ingredients for the second pizza.

Top with fresh basil and serve!

NOTE: Pat the tomatoes dry to keep the pizza from getting soggy.

CHICKEN FAJITA QUICHE

YIELD: 6 SERVINGS

I'm a sucker for a good quiche. It's kind of the perfect meal, whether it's for breakfast, brunch, lunch or dinner. I was given *the best quiche* recipe at my bridal shower from my Aunt Rhonda. On her recipe card she wrote, "Real men eat quiche. Your uncle loves this recipe!" I was sold.

I have probably made 50 different versions of her basic quiche recipe over the past 10 years, and loved every single one of them. This particular quiche has a fajita flair, and if you're feeling creative, make a fun bell pepper design on the top like I did.

1 pie crust, unbaked

1 cup (125 g) diced rotisserie chicken

½ cup (118 ml) milk

½ cup (118 g) light mayonnaise

3 large eggs

4 tsp (13 g) cornstarch

6 oz (170 g) shredded Mexican blend cheese

½ onion, diced

1 bell pepper, diced, feel free to use more than one color

¼ tsp cumin

¼ tsp chili powder

¼ tsp garlic powder

½ tsp salt

½ tsp fresh ground back pepper

Preheat the oven to 400°F (205°C).

Place the pie shell on a baking sheet. This makes taking it out of the oven a breeze.

Whisk all the ingredients together in a large bowl and pour into the pie shell. Bake for 30 minutes, or just until the top of the quiche is light brown.

Let the quiche rest for at least 15 minutes before slicing and serving.

NOTE: If you want to add a design to the top of your quiche, just add the bell pepper strips after you've poured the mixture into the pie shell.

CHICKEN MADEIRA WITH ROASTED ASPARAGUS

YIELD: 4 SERVINGS OR 2 LARGE SERVINGS

This is truly a remarkable and impressive dinner that is so simple to prepare. It takes about 30 minutes from start to finish, but there's not a whole lot of work involved. If you've never had Madeira chicken before, you're in for a treat. The chicken is drenched in a wine sauce made with Madeira, a Portuguese wine that adds incredible flavor to this dish. It's a lot like Marsala but even more flavorful—it's fantastic!

2 tbsp (29 g) butter

2 tbsp (30 ml) extra virgin olive oil, divided

8 oz (227 g) sliced white mushrooms

2 cups (480 ml) Madeira wine

1 (14 ½ oz [411 g]) can reduced-sodium beef broth

1 (10 ½ oz [298 g]) can beef consommé

8 oz (227 g) fresh asparagus tips, rinsed and patted dry

Salt and pepper, to taste

2 rotisserie chicken breasts, thickly sliced

4 oz (113 g) shredded mozzarella cheese

Preheat the oven to 400°F (205°C).

Heat a large sauté pan over medium heat. Add the butter and 1 tablespoon (15 ml) of the olive oil and heat until the butter has melted. Add the sliced mushrooms and stir to coat. Sauté until lightly browned and fragrant, about 4 to 5 minutes.

Add the Madeira wine, beef broth and consommé and bring to a boil. Reduce the heat and continue cooking until the liquids have reduced by half. The liquid won't thicken, but the flavor will be intensified. This takes about 20 minutes.

While the wine and broth mixture is simmering away, place the asparagus tips on a baking sheet. Drizzle the remaining 1 tablespoon (15 ml) olive oil over the top and season with salt and pepper. Toss gently to evenly distribute the oil. Roast for 10 to 15 minutes, or until the asparagus is tender but still slightly crisp. Check at about 10 minutes because it really depends on the size of your asparagus.

Add the sliced chicken breasts to the sauté pan and spoon the sauce over the chicken. Top with the shredded cheese. Place a lid over the pan so the cheese melts.

Plate the sliced chicken and top with asparagus and more sauce. *To. Die. For.*

CHICKEN, SHRIMP AND ANDOUILLE JAMBALAYA IN A JIFFY

YIELD: 6 SERVINGS

Right now you're probably thinking that I'm a little bit crazy. *Jambalaya? Easy?* You betcha. Sure, it takes a few ingredients, but this recipe makes the most delicious jambalaya in a jiffy.

Packed full with amazing flavors from the chicken, shrimp and andouille sausage, this jambalaya is a meat lover's dream come true!

2 tbsp (29 g) butter

1 large onion, diced

3 green onions, thinly sliced

½ red bell pepper, diced

½ green bell pepper, diced

2 tsp (10 g) Cajun seasoning

1 tsp oregano leaves

1 tsp ground thyme

¼ tsp salt

½ tsp (5 g) fresh ground black pepper

12 oz (340 g) Cajun-style andouille sausage, sliced

2 cups (250 g) diced rotisserie chicken

4 cloves garlic, minced

3 cups (710 ml) low-sodium chicken broth

1 (14 ½ oz [411 g]) can fire-roasted diced tomatoes

1 ½ cups (241 g) long-grain rice

12 oz (340 g) large raw shrimp, peeled and deveined

Melt the butter in a large pot with a lid. Add the onion, green onions and bell peppers and cook over medium-high heat for 5 to 6 minutes, or until the onion is translucent.

Stir in the Cajun seasoning, oregano, thyme, salt and pepper. Add the andouille sausage and chicken and cook for another 3 to 4 minutes. Add the garlic and cook for 1 minute.

Stir in the chicken broth, tomatoes and rice and bring to a boil. Place the lid on the pot and reduce the heat to low. Simmer for 20 minutes, or until the rice is fully cooked.

Remove the lid and tuck the shrimp into the rice. Cover and cook for another 4 to 5 minutes, or until the shrimp are nice and pink. Remove the pot from the heat and top with additional sliced green onions and hot sauce, if desired.

Serve immediately.

CHEESY CHICKEN TAMALES

YIELD: 30 TAMALES

You're probably surprised to see a recipe for tamales in a cookbook for easy family dinners, but I urge you to give it a try, as it's one of my family's favorites.

I've made the somewhat lengthy process of making tamales easier by combining the tamale dough with the filling. I love making tamales like this because you are guaranteed delicious flavor in every single bite. Read through the directions twice before starting, and you'll be good to go!

1 (8 oz [226 g]) package dried cornhusks, you won't use the entire package

2 cups (303 g) masa

¼ cup (57 g) butter, softened

2 tsp (8 g) baking powder

1 tsp salt

2 cups (480 ml) low-sodium chicken broth

1 ½ cups (190 g) shredded rotisserie chicken

4 oz (110 ml) enchilada sauce

4 oz (113 g) shredded Monterey Jack OR pepper jack cheese

3 green onions, thinly sliced

Soak the cornhusks in very hot water until pliable, about 30 to 35 minutes. They will try to float to the top, so place a can on top of them to keep them from doing so.

Combine the masa, butter, baking powder and salt in a large mixing bowl. Mix until thoroughly combined. Add the broth, ½ cup (118 ml) at a time, until a soft dough forms. The dough will be a little sticky, but you should be able to handle it with ease.

Combine the chicken and enchilada sauce in a small bowl and stir with a fork until the chicken is nicely coated. Stir the chicken, cheese and green onions into the masa dough.

Remove four cornhusks from the water and tear into strips. These will be used to tie up the tamales.

Now comes the fun part! Pull out a large baking sheet or cutting board to work on. Remove the husks from the water and pat dry. Place one husk in front of you with the narrow end of the triangle facing towards you.

Spoon about ¼ cup (60 g) of the filling onto the center of the husk. Fold up the narrow end to the center of the filling and fold the two sides in over the filling. Use a strip to tie the top closed. Set the tamale aside and repeat until all of the filling is used. I made about 30 tamales.

Place the tamales in a steamer basket, cover and cook for 40 minutes. Let the tamales stand for a few minutes before serving.

My boys eat these tamales like they're candy bars. I'm a little more sophisticated and enjoy my tamales with salsa and sour cream or Mexican crema.

CHICKEN ZUCCHINI STUFFED SHELLS

YIELD: 6 SERVINGS

Zucchini happens to be my favorite squash, and we grow it in abundance each year in our garden. I make everything with zucchini—including cookies and cake—but these shells are something special. Each one is stuffed to the brim with a flavorful ricotta-based filling that is dreamily creamy. The basil is the star of the show and adds freshness to the dish. My boys eat these with their hands (I know, it's terrible!), so I guess forks are optional?

1 medium zucchini

1 (15 oz [425 g]) container part-skim ricotta

⅓ cup (13 g) chopped fresh basil

1 cup (125 g) diced rotisserie chicken

1 egg, lightly beaten

½ tsp salt

½ tsp fresh ground black pepper

12 oz (340 g) jumbo pasta shells, cooked

1 (24 oz [680 g]) jar marinara OR pasta sauce

4 oz (113 g) shredded mozzarella cheese

2 oz (57 g) grated Parmesan cheese

Preheat the oven to 400°F (205°C).

Grate the zucchini onto a paper towel–lined plate, wrap it with the paper towels and squeeze dry.

Combine the grated zucchini, ricotta, basil, chicken, egg, salt and pepper in a medium bowl and mix to combine.

Transfer the mixture to a large resealable bag and cut one corner off it. Use the bag to pipe the filling into the shells, or you can also just spoon the filling into the shells.

Lightly spray a 9" x 13" (23 x 33 cm) baking dish with nonstick cooking spray.

Spread about 1 cup (230 ml) of the marinara sauce onto the bottom of the dish and place the filled shells on top. Pour the remaining marinara sauce over the shells.

Sprinkle the mozzarella and Parmesan cheese on top of the sauce. Cover the baking dish with foil and bake for 30 minutes. Remove the foil and bake for another 4 to 5 minutes, or until the cheese is bubbling and lightly browned. Sprinkle with additional fresh basil, if desired.

NOTE: If you prefer, this recipe can be made with manicotti instead. Just follow the directions as written, using manicotti in place of the shells.

ROTISSERIE CHICKEN PAN GRAVY

YIELD: 4 SERVINGS

As much as I love the rotisserie chicken on its own, there's just something about chicken with gravy that I find irresistible. One of my all-time favorite meals is a juicy rotisserie chicken breast topped with creamy gravy and served with a side of mashed potatoes. Oh yeah, and a side salad with bleu cheese dressing. Heaven!

The drippings that you'll find at the bottom of your rotisserie chicken container are what I like to call liquid gold. If you've chilled your chicken, you'll notice that the drippings have set up into a gel-like consistency. No problem. You can either heat the container to turn them back into liquid or scrape it all out.

The drippings are the perfect start to this simple gravy. They add an incredible amount of flavor. I use the Slow Cooker Chicken Broth (page 124) recipe in this book, but store-bought broth will work just as well.

Drippings from 1 or 2 rotisserie chickens

3 tbsp (43 g) butter

¼ cup (31 g) all-purpose flour

1 ½ cups (355 ml) chicken broth

Salt and pepper, to taste

Add the drippings and butter to a medium skillet. Heat over medium heat until the butter has melted.

Whisk in the flour and cook for 1 to 2 minutes. Gradually add the chicken broth and whisk to combine. Keep in mind that if the broth is heated, this process goes much faster.

Bring the gravy to a simmer over medium heat, stirring frequently. Continue cooking until the gravy has reached your desired consistency. Season with salt and pepper, if needed.

NOTE: Although I love adding a generous amount of pepper to this recipe, I find that salt is rarely needed. Rotisserie chickens are typically heavily seasoned, which results in very flavorful drippings that are pretty salty to begin with. Check for seasoning before you add any salt and pepper.

CHAPTER 7

SAVORY SANDWICHES

I grew up on sandwiches. I kind of thought they were boring, but now as an adult, I have found that sandwiches have much more to offer than I originally thought possible.

Sure, a sandwich can be super simple: two pieces of bread with some meat and cheese in the middle. But it can also become the ultimate comfort food as well—think grilled cheese! And for those of us who enjoy it, a little "fancy" as well.

The incredible, edible sandwich is the meal that everyone loves to sink their teeth into! What I love best about sandwiches is the variety. From the dozens of types of bread, to the layers and layers of flavor and texture, every sandwich has the ability to be unique and interesting. Don't just stop at the mayo, mustard, lettuce and tomato—there's so much more out there!

What you don't want to miss: Chicken Cordon Bleu Pull-Apart Sandwich (page 153), Blackberry Brie Grilled Cheese Sandwich (page 154) and the Parmesan-Crusted Pesto Grilled Cheese Sandwich (page 165).

CHICKEN CORDON BLEU PULL-APART SANDWICH

YIELD: 6 SERVINGS

It took a tremendous amount of willpower for me to not make half of this book about chicken cordon bleu. It's my most favorite dish EVER. But I couldn't resist this pull-apart sandwich. It's ridiculously simple and outrageously divine. It's also a great starting point for making a ton of variations of this sandwich. If you want to add produce like lettuce and tomatoes, just do so after the sandwich has been baked.

1 loaf French bread

4 oz (113 g) thinly sliced Gruyere or Swiss cheese

1 rotisserie chicken breast, thinly sliced

7 oz (198 g) thinly sliced black forest ham

Dijon mustard, optional

Preheat the oven to 350°F (177°C).

Cut slits on the top of the bread that come down to the very bottom of the loaf, but NOT through it. You want to leave a sort of hinge there to keep it all together, but it should also be easy to pull apart.

In every other space, place a slice of cheese, some chicken and a slice of ham. You want to be careful not to overfill, or you will end up with a circle sandwich instead of a loaf. It should be: bread, cheese, chicken, ham, bread, bread, cheese, chicken, ham, bread, bread. . . . If you want to, spread some Dijon mustard onto one slice of bread per sandwich.

Wrap the sandwich tightly in foil and bake for 20 minutes. Remove the foil and bake for an additional 5 minutes, or until the cheese is nice and melted.

Pull apart the sandwiches and enjoy!

NOTE: Pull-apart sandwiches can also be made on the grill or BBQ during hot summer months. Just place the foil-wrapped sandwich away from direct heat, and you're good to go!

BLACKBERRY BRIE GRILLED CHEESE SANDWICH

YIELD: 4 SANDWICHES

This is the perfect gourmet grilled cheese sandwich with mouthwatering Brie cheese, all melted and ooey gooey! This is my favorite sandwich of the entire book. While the flavors are a little "grown-up," the sandwich can easily be altered to please a child's palate. Substitute the Brie with provolone or mozzarella, and your kids will go crazy. But have them try it with Brie first!

The blackberry preserves are the perfect sweet counterpart to the rich Brie cheese. It takes this sandwich from just good to something irresistible. If you can't find blackberry, try strawberry or fig instead—both are delightful on this sandwich!

¼ cup (57 g) butter, softened

8 slices sourdough or French bread

8 oz (227 g) Brie cheese, thinly sliced

2 rotisserie chicken breasts, thinly sliced

1 tsp herbes de Provence

¼ cup (59 ml) blackberry preserves or fruit spread

Butter the outside of one slice of bread and place on a grill pan or skillet preheated over medium heat. Layer the Brie and chicken on the bread and sprinkle with some of the herbes de Provence.

Smear 1 tablespoon (15 ml) of the blackberry preserves on another slice of bread and place on top of the chicken. Butter the outside of the top slice of bread. Grill each side for 4 to 5 minutes, or just until the bread turns golden brown.

Repeat for the remaining sandwiches. Serve hot.

CHICKEN DILLY CROISSANWICH

YIELD: 4 SANDWICHES

Our family went on a cruise while I was in the process of writing this book. On the cruise, we enjoyed these amazing chicken dill sliders that had us all saying, "Mmmm!" I knew I could re-create them at home, and we've been making them ever since. Every time I pull these sandwiches together, it makes me think of our fun family time together, and they taste that much better!

I am partial to croissants for this sandwich, but you can use whatever bread you have on hand.

2 cups (250 g) diced rotisserie chicken

2 tbsp (6 g) minced fresh dill

½ cup (118 ml) plain Greek yogurt

¼ cup (59 ml) mayonnaise

1 lemon, juiced

Salt and pepper, to taste

Butter lettuce

4 croissants, cut in half

Combine the chicken, dill, yogurt, mayonnaise and lemon juice in a medium bowl. Season with salt and pepper to taste.

Spoon onto a lettuce-lined croissant or bread of your choice. Enjoy!

CHICKEN REUBEN PANINI SANDWICHES

YIELD: 4 SANDWICHES

I love taking a classic sandwich and putting a chicken spin on it. I did just that with the Reuben. These paninis couldn't be easier to make and are full of the classic Reuben flavor.

I used a marbled rye bread for these sandwiches, and I just love the drama it adds—so fun! The rotisserie chicken keeps the workload down to a minimum and adds great flavor to the sandwich. Keep it simple and serve with some salty potato chips for the win!

8 slices marbled rye bread

8 slices Swiss cheese

2 rotisserie chicken breasts, thinly sliced

1 (16 oz [454 g]) package sauerkraut, drained and squeezed dry

1 oz (27 g) Thousand Island dressing

2 tbsp (29 g) butter, softened

Preheat a panini press or grill pan.

Place a piece of Swiss cheese on each of four slices of rye bread. Divide the chicken evenly and place it on top of the cheese.

In a small bowl, combine the sauerkraut and Thousand Island dressing. Use a fork to toss together and to evenly coat the sauerkraut with the dressing. Spoon the sauerkraut mixture over the top of the chicken. Top with the remaining cheese and bread.

Thinly spread a little butter on each side of the sandwich before placing in the press or grill.

Grill for 2 to 3 minutes on each side, until the cheese is melted and the bread is golden brown.

Serve immediately!

NOTE: The most important step in this recipe is making sure all of the liquid is squeezed out of the sauerkraut. Nothing worse than a soggy panini!

HAWAIIAN CHICKEN SANDWICHES

YIELD: 4 SANDWICHES

Bringing the tropics to your home . . . in a sandwich! This sandwich is so unique and delicious that it deserves a special bun. I like to use an onion bun for mine, but a Hawaiian roll would be ideal as well. You're going to love the juicy sweetness of the pineapple in every bite!

¼ cup (59 ml) teriyaki sauce

2 rotisserie chicken breasts, thinly sliced

4 slices provolone cheese

Lettuce

4 buns

4 pineapple slices, canned or fresh is fine

Tomato slices

Heat the teriyaki sauce in a small skillet over medium heat. Add the chicken slices to the skillet and flip to coat. Cook for 4 to 5 minutes, or until the chicken is heated through.

Group the chicken into four bun-size piles and top with a slice of provolone cheese. Put a lid on the skillet and continue cooking until the cheese has melted, about 4 to 5 minutes.

Place a piece of lettuce on the bottom half of each bun and place the chicken and cheese on top. Top with a slice of pineapple, more lettuce and a tomato slice. You can add more teriyaki sauce, if you'd like.

Place the top bun on and serve immediately.

MEXICAN TORTAS

YIELD: 4 TORTAS

I had my first torta just last year. I'm hooked. The torta bread is just so incredibly soft, chewy and fabulous! You can pretty much put anything you want in a torta, but I love this chicken and salsa version. It takes about five minutes to pull together four sandwiches. Since you'll have some extra time, why not whip up some fresh guacamole and serve with crispy tortilla chips? YUM!

2 cups (250 g) shredded rotisserie chicken

½ cup (118 ml) salsa

1 (16 oz [454 g]) can refried beans, you won't need the entire can

4 torta rolls

4 oz (113 g) shredded Mexican blend cheese

Shredded lettuce

1 tomato, thinly sliced

1 avocado, gently smashed

Combine the chicken and salsa in a microwave-safe bowl. Heat on high, in 30-second increments, until the chicken is heated through. Depending on the microwave, it should take 1 to 2 minutes.

Spread the refried beans onto the bottom half of each roll. Top with the salsa-chicken mixture, cheese, lettuce and tomato.

Spread the smashed avocado on the top half of each roll and put the sandwich together. Done!

PARMESAN-CRUSTED PESTO GRILLED CHEESE SANDWICH

YIELD: 4 SANDWICHES

If you're looking for a grilled cheese sandwich that is going to blow you away, this is it, hands down. There are a number of components to this sandwich, and you actually build them on the grill. Both sides of the sandwich are coated in Parmesan and then grilled to golden brown perfection. My mouth is watering just thinking about it! Pesto, mozzarella and spinach—this sandwich has it all!

¼ cup (57 g) butter, softened

8 slices sourdough bread

½ cup (90 g) grated Parmesan cheese

8 oz (227 g) thinly sliced mozzarella cheese

2 rotisserie chicken breasts, thinly sliced

Baby spinach

¼ cup (59 ml) pesto

Heat a skillet or griddle to medium. Spread butter on four slices of bread.

Add the Parmesan cheese to a shallow plate and press the buttered side of each slice into the cheese, forming a thin layer of cheese on top of the butter.

Lay those four slices of bread on the skillet or griddle. Cover the slices with half of the mozzarella cheese, followed by the chicken and a single layer of baby spinach leaves. Top with the remaining half of the mozzarella cheese.

Spread butter on the four remaining slices of bread and press into the grated Parmesan, as we did before. Carefully spread 1 tablespoon (15 ml) of pesto on the opposite side of each slice of bread and place on top of the sandwich, with the Parmesan side exposed.

Flip once the Parmesan has turned a golden brown, usually a good 7 to 8 minutes. Don't rush yourself while building the sandwiches. You've got plenty of time.

After flipping the sandwiches, grill the second side for another 7 to 8 minutes. Again, you're looking for that golden crust.

Cut in half and serve.

ROTISSERIE CHICKEN SALAD SANDWICH

YIELD: 4 SANDWICHES

This sandwich was one of the very first rotisserie chicken recipes I put on my blog. My mom made the most amazing chicken salad sandwiches growing up, and this was how she made them, minus the rotisserie chicken. Diced fresh apples are absolutely delightful to bite into. That sweet crunch gives so much character and flavor to this sandwich.

2 cups (250 g) diced rotisserie chicken

1 apple, diced, I use Gala

½ cup (76 g) raisins

¼ cup (59 g) light mayonnaise

1 tsp celery seed

Salt and pepper, to taste

8 slices of the bread of your choice

Combine all ingredients except the bread in a bowl and stir until the mayonnaise is evenly incorporated. Chill for at least 30 minutes.

Serve on your choice of bread with lettuce or sprouts. Simple and delicious!

CHICKEN RANCH BLAT WRAP

YIELD: 4 WRAPS

BLAT = bacon, lettuce, avocado and tomato. Yep, you want this. This quick wrap is packed, and I mean PACKED, with incredible flavor and crunch. The ranch dressing goes beautifully with the scrumptious rotisserie chicken, crunchy bacon and creamy avocado. The sweet freshness of the tomato is the perfect addition. I like to use flavored wraps or tortillas for this recipe. They add a fun punch of color and flavor to the dish.

½ cup (118 ml) ranch dressing

4 large wraps or tortillas

Lettuce or spinach

2 rotisserie chicken breasts, thinly sliced

8 slices bacon, cooked and cut into 1 inch (2.5 cm) pieces

1 avocado, thinly sliced

1 tomato, thinly sliced

Spread 2 tablespoons (30 ml) of ranch dressing on each wrap or tortilla and place a single layer of lettuce or spinach right on top. Layer with chicken, bacon, avocado and tomato, evenly dividing among the four wraps.

Fold in the ends and roll up just like a burrito. Make sure to roll it up tightly! Cut in half and serve immediately.

SLOPPY JOE-ANNE'S

YIELD: 4 SANDWICHES

This recipe almost didn't happen. I was a little nervous about how my boys would feel about sloppy joes made with chicken . . . so different! I honestly couldn't have been happier with the result. They LOVED them so much that this is now our preferred way to enjoy sloppy joes, and they are SO much healthier.

Side note: I totally wanted to call these Sloppy Chicks, but my friend Ann suggested Sloppy Joe-Anne's instead. She was right.

1 tbsp (15 ml) olive oil

1 small yellow onion, diced

2 cloves garlic, minced

2 cups (250 g) finely diced rotisserie chicken

1 (14 ½ oz [411 g]) can diced tomatoes, drained

⅓ cup (79 ml) ketchup

2 tbsp (30 ml) Worcestershire sauce

4 hamburger buns

Heat the oil over medium-high heat in a medium sauté pan.

Add the diced onion to the pan, reduce the heat to medium and cook, stirring frequently, until the onion is soft and translucent, about 4 to 5 minutes. Add the minced garlic and cook for an additional 1 minute, stirring frequently.

Stir in the diced chicken, tomatoes, ketchup and Worcestershire sauce and bring to a simmer.

Continue cooking the mixture at a gentle simmer until the sauce is reduced by half. This will take about 15 minutes.

Divide the filling evenly among the four buns and serve immediately. These sandwiches are especially delightful on toasted buns.

TZATZIKI CHICKEN SALAD PITA POCKETS

YIELD: 4 PITA POCKETS

Pita pockets are all kinds of fun, and we'll put almost anything inside them. These tzatziki chicken pockets are a personal favorite of mine. I kind of feel like I'm at a spa when I'm eating these—the cucumber and mint are so refreshing and light. I definitely feel like a million bucks when I'm done devouring mine.

1 cup (237 ml) plain Greek yogurt

2 cups (250 g) diced rotisserie chicken

½ English cucumber, seeded and diced

½ red onion, diced

3 tbsp (9 g) fresh dill, chopped

3 tbsp (8 g) fresh mint, chopped

1 clove garlic, minced

Salt and pepper, to taste

2 pita pockets, cut in half

Lettuce

Sliced tomatoes

Combine the yogurt, chicken, cucumber, red onion, dill, mint, garlic, salt and pepper in a medium bowl and gently stir to combine.

Spoon the filling into each pita pocket with some lettuce leaves and a slice of tomato tucked inside.

Serve immediately.

GRILLED CALIFORNIA CHICKEN CLUB

YIELD: 4 SANDWICHES

Because I've lived in California my whole life, there is a certain set of ingredients that really says California to me. Sour cream, avocado, Swiss cheese and bacon is one such set. I think you'll be surprised at how much you DON'T miss the mayonnaise in this sandwich. The sour cream is lighter, fresher and just a bit tart. You may find yourself using sour cream in all of your sandwiches after this!

8 slices sourdough bread

¼ cup (57 g) butter

4 slices Swiss cheese

8 slices bacon, cooked

2 rotisserie chicken breasts, thinly sliced

¼ cup (59 ml) sour cream

1 avocado, thinly sliced

1 tomato, thinly sliced

Lettuce

Heat a large skillet over medium-high heat. Butter four slices of the bread and place on the skillet. Depending on how big your skillet is, it may be necessary to make the sandwiches in batches.

Place a slice of Swiss cheese on top of each bread slice, followed by the bacon and chicken. Top with the remaining slices of bread and butter each top.

Reduce the heat to medium and grill each side for 4 to 5 minutes, or just until the bread turns golden brown.

Remove the sandwich and open them up. Spread sour cream on the piece of bread that doesn't have the cheese. Add the avocado, tomato and lettuce. Replace the top slices and serve immediately.

CHAPTER 8

SENSATIONAL SALADS

There are so many nights when the family gets home after a late swim practice or a fun-filled party and all we really want is a salad. Something easy, something fresh and something fabulous.

Chicken Artichoke Pizza Pasta Salad (page 177), Layered Chicken Taco Salad (page 185) and the Southwest Chicken Caesar Salad (page 189) all make frequent appearances at our home. Just remember, salads are anything but boring.

CHICKEN ARTICHOKE PIZZA PASTA SALAD

YIELD: 6 SERVINGS

This salad is one of those recipes that you can make ahead of time and pull out at a moment's notice. It's well received at parties, and it's the perfect summertime fare. Cool and comforting, this salad is packed with bright punches of flavor from the artichokes and sun-dried tomatoes. Everyone always manages to scoop a few extra fresh mozzarella balls onto their plate during serving time, and who can blame them!

¼ cup (59 ml) extra virgin olive oil

⅓ cup (80 ml) rice vinegar

16 oz (454 g) bow-tie, penne or shell pasta, cooked

4 oz (114 g) chopped oil-packed sun-dried tomatoes, drained

1 (14 ¾ oz [418 g]) container marinated artichokes, drained and chopped

8 oz (226 g) bite-size fresh mozzarella, halved

½ red onion, thinly sliced

2 cups (250 g) diced rotisserie chicken

½ cup (13 g) fresh basil, julienned

2 tbsp (5 g) fresh oregano, chopped

Salt and pepper, to taste

Whisk the olive oil and rice vinegar together in a small bowl until emulsified.

Combine all other ingredients in a large bowl and drizzle the dressing on top, tossing to thoroughly coat all ingredients.

Refrigerate for at least 1 hour before serving so the flavors have time to develop.

CHICKEN POPPY SEED SALAD PUFFS

YIELD: 8 SERVINGS

I adore a good poppy seed salad, especially when presented in these adorable puff pastry cups! I made the salad a bit healthier with the use of Greek yogurt rather than mayonnaise, in hopes to offset the pastry puff. The grapes are a must-have here; their pop of juicy sweetness MAKES the recipe. Feel free to toast the almonds or leave them raw—both ways are excellent!

This recipe can easily be halved if you don't need 18 puffs. No biggie!

1 (17 ⅓ oz [490 g]) package puff pastry, thawed according to package directions

2 cups (250 g) diced rotisserie chicken

2 stalks celery, diced

1 cup (237 ml) plain Greek yogurt

8 oz (227 g) purple grapes, halved

6 oz (170 g) slivered almonds, toasted if you'd like

1 tbsp (8 g) poppy seeds

1 tsp dill weed

Preheat the oven to 400°F (205°C).

Gently roll out the puff pastry on a lightly floured surface. Cut each puff pastry sheet into 9 squares, for a total of 18 squares.

Lightly spray a muffin tin with nonstick cooking spray.

Press each square into the muffin tin and poke holes on the bottom with a fork. You will either need to use two muffin tins or bake two batches of the puff pastry. Bake puffs for 13 to 15 minutes, or until golden brown. The centers of the puffs might, well, puff. Use the bottom of a wooden spoon to flatten the centers if needed. Let the puffs cool for a couple of minutes before removing them from the tin to a cooling rack.

While the puffs are baking, combine the chicken, celery, Greek yogurt, grapes, almonds, poppy seeds and dill weed in a large bowl. Stir gently to coat all ingredients with the yogurt.

Spoon the chicken salad into each puff and top with additional toasted almonds for garnish. So pretty!

CHINESE CHICKEN SALAD

YIELD: 4 SERVINGS

Boom! Make this for dinner tonight, and you're going to have a new favorite to add to your rotation! It's just about the easiest recipe ever, and it tastes light but is wonderfully filling. Packed full of fresh veggies like red bell pepper, cucumber and snow peas, this salad is both pretty to look at and yummy to eat.

This recipe is inspired by my Aunt Rene's Chinese Chicken Salad, and it will NOT disappoint!

1 tsp salt

5 oz (142 g) angel hair pasta, broken in half

6 oz (170 g) snow peas, strings removed and cut diagonally

3 green onions, thinly sliced

2 cups (250 g) shredded rotisserie chicken, both white and dark meat is good here

1 red bell pepper, seeded, deveined and diced

1 English cucumber, seeded and diced

3 tbsp (44 ml) teriyaki sauce

2 tbsp (30 ml) rice vinegar

2 tsp (10 ml) sesame oil

2 tsp (7 g) sesame seeds, toasted

½ tsp kosher salt

¼ tsp fresh ground black pepper

Boil 4 quarts (3.6 L) of water and the salt in a medium pot. Add the angel hair pasta and cook for 2 minutes, then add the snow peas and cook for an additional 1 minute.

Remove from the heat immediately and pour the pasta and peas into a strainer, drain and rinse with cold water for 1 minute. Transfer to a large bowl.

Add the green onions, chicken, red bell pepper and cucumber to the bowl and set aside.

Whisk together the teriyaki sauce, rice vinegar, sesame oil, sesame seeds, salt and black pepper in a small bowl. Pour over the pasta mixture and gently toss.

This salad can be refrigerated or served immediately. Top with additional sliced green onions and sesame seeds if you're in the mood.

NOTE: Cut the English cucumber in half lengthwise and run a spoon down its center to remove the seeds quickly and easily.

CURRIED CHICKEN SALAD

YIELD: 4 SERVINGS

My mom loved a good curried chicken salad. We used to go to this little deli off of the highway for lunch, and every time we went, my mom would order the curried chicken salad. I remember thinking that it didn't look all that appetizing, but years later, I'm a curry nut. I wish my mom was still around to enjoy this delicious salad with me. I make mine just as I remember hers, with cashews and golden raisins.

You might think curry is a bit grown up, but the sweetness of the raisins ensures that kids of all ages enjoy this salad. My boys and I enjoy it best on buttery crackers—sooo good!

2 cups (250 g) diced rotisserie chicken

½ cup (118 ml) Greek yogurt

1 tsp curry powder

2 green onions, thinly sliced

½ cup (76 g) golden raisins

½ cup (56 g) whole roasted cashews

Salt and pepper, to taste

Combine all of the ingredients in a medium bowl and mix well to combine.

Spread onto bread or serve with crackers, or eat with a spoon. You just can't go wrong here.

LAYERED CHICKEN TACO SALAD

YIELD: 6 SERVINGS

This gorgeous salad has been a family favorite for years! It's a lot of fun to assemble and even more so to eat. I like to serve this salad in a large trifle bowl so everyone can admire my handiwork with the layers.

2 romaine lettuce hearts, chopped

8 oz (227 g) shredded Mexican blend cheese

2 cups (250 g) diced rotisserie chicken

1 (15 oz [425 g]) can black beans, rinsed and drained

1 (15 ¼ oz [432 g]) can sweet corn, drained

Tortilla chips

2 Roma tomatoes, chopped

2 avocados, diced

Green onions, sliced

½ cup (118 ml) salsa, whatever your favorite kind is

½ cup (118 ml) ranch dressing

Divide the lettuce and cheese into three equal portions, and divide the chicken in half.

Layer the ingredients, starting from the bottom, as such: lettuce, cheese, beans, chicken, lettuce, cheese, corn, chicken, lettuce, cheese, chips, tomatoes, avocados and green onions.

Combine the salsa and ranch in a small bowl and stir to combine. Drizzle on top of the salad.

Serve with more tortilla chips.

LEMON CHICKEN COUSCOUS SALAD

YIELD: 4 SERVINGS

Couscous is one of those ingredients that I didn't discover until after college. Once discovered, however, it quickly became a staple in my kitchen. Its preparation is quick and easy, and it adds the most delightful texture to any recipe.

This salad is one of my very favorites; it is both light and filling at the same time. Fresh tomatoes, red onion, artichokes and lemon zest guarantee both brightness and freshness in every bite. The dressing is a breeze to prepare and is just what this couscous salad needs.

FOR THE DRESSING

1 lemon, zested

2 lemons, juiced

1 clove garlic, minced

¼ cup (10 g) minced fresh Italian parsley

¼ tsp fresh ground black pepper

⅓ cup (79 ml) extra virgin olive oil

FOR THE SALAD

1 cup (240 ml) water

1 cup (240 ml) low-sodium chicken broth

1 tbsp (15 ml) extra virgin olive oil

10 oz (284 g) couscous

1 English cucumber, thinly sliced

1 red onion, thinly sliced

14 oz (396 g) quartered artichoke hearts, drained

6 oz (170 g) feta cheese

2 cups (250 g) diced chicken

1 pint (322 g) cherry or grape tomatoes, halved

Butter lettuce leaves

Combine all of the dressing ingredients in a small Mason jar. Tighten the lid and shake for 1 minute or so, until emulsified. Then, set aside.

Bring the water, chicken broth and olive oil to a boil in a medium saucepan. Stir in the couscous, turn off the heat and cover. Let the couscous sit, undisturbed, for about 5 to 6 minutes. This is when the magic happens.

Remove the lid and fluff the couscous with a fork. Let the couscous cool for about 10 minutes.

Combine the couscous, cucumber, red onion, artichoke hearts, feta cheese, chicken and tomatoes in a large serving bowl. Drizzle the dressing and gently mix to combine. It's really more of a fluffing and folding action, rather than mixing. Just be gentle with the ingredients.

Serve with fresh lettuce leaves OR serve on top of lettuce leaves to make couscous salad cups—so fun for parties!

SOUTHWEST CHICKEN CAESAR SALAD

YIELD: 4 SERVINGS

I'm a big fan of Caesar salads. This was my go-to salad when study sessions ran late in high school and college, and I've found out over the years that it's even better when you add some southwest flair to it. This recipe makes use of store-bought Caesar dressing, and with a couple additions, you've got an amazing southwest-flavored Caesar dressing with just a little bit of a kick. Make sure to use your favorite salsa to ensure a flavor you'll love!

4 oz (110 ml) refrigerated Caesar dressing

1 lime, juiced

½ tsp ground cumin

4 oz (113 ml) salsa, your favorite brand

9 oz (255 g) romaine hearts, chopped

2 cups (250 g) diced rotisserie chicken

3 ½ oz (99 g) tri-color tortilla strips

5 oz (142 g) Cotija cheese, crumbled

Whisk together the Caesar dressing, lime juice, cumin and salsa in a small bowl. Then, set aside.

Place chopped romaine hearts in a large serving bowl. Top with the chicken, tortilla strips and Cotija. Toss with the dressing and serve immediately.

NOTE: The tortilla strips are what make this salad fun for the whole family. You can find them next to the croutons and other salad toppings at your local grocery store.

STRAWBERRY SPINACH SALAD WITH BALSAMIC HONEY VINAIGRETTE

YIELD: 4 SERVINGS

The homemade balsamic honey vinaigrette is the key to this tasty salad, and it's made the old-fashioned way—in a jar! It's super easy, and any extra dressing can just be popped into the fridge when you're done.

I love balsamic SO MUCH, and I especially love it on this salad with chicken and strawberries. I made this version with toasted pecans and Gorgonzola cheese, two of my favorites!

¼ cup (60 ml) balsamic vinegar, get the good stuff!

1 tbsp (15 g) Dijon mustard

1 tbsp (15 ml) honey or agave nectar

½ shallot, minced

Salt and pepper, to taste

½ cup (118 ml) extra virgin olive oil

5 oz (142 g) fresh baby spinach

2 rotisserie chicken breasts, sliced

1 pint (303 g) fresh strawberries, hulled and sliced

½ cup (60 g) chopped toasted pecans, walnuts or almonds

2 oz (57 g) Gorgonzola cheese, crumbled, or feta, goat, blue, etc.

Combine the balsamic vinegar, Dijon mustard, honey, shallot, salt, pepper and olive oil in a Mason jar. Now shake, shake, shake until the dressing has emulsified. I learned this trick from my Nana! This recipe makes more than you will need for this particular salad, so save the rest and just give it a good shake before using it next time.

Place the spinach in a large salad bowl and top with the chicken, strawberries, pecans and cheese. Serve with the balsamic honey vinaigrette.

WALNUT CRANBERRY GORGONZOLA SALAD

YIELD: 6 SERVINGS

Every single ingredient in this salad packs a punch. The arugula has a peppery bite that is offset by the sweetness of the dried cranberries. The Gorgonzola adds a tang and creaminess, while the chopped walnuts add the oh-so-necessary crunch factor. The rotisserie chicken complements every single other ingredient in this salad, and when topped with a high-quality balsamic vinaigrette, this salad is absolute perfection.

5 oz (142 g) baby arugula

2 cups (250 g) diced rotisserie chicken

½ cup (50 g) dried cranberries

4 oz (113 g) crumbled Gorgonzola

½ cup (58 g) chopped toasted walnuts

Balsamic vinaigrette, to taste

Divide the arugula among four bowls. Top with the chicken, cranberries, Gorgonzola and toasted walnuts. Serve with your favorite balsamic vinaigrette.

CHICKEN, BACON AND RANCH PASTA SALAD

YIELD: 8 SERVINGS

This is one of my favorite summertime salads. It's light, pretty and perfect for a picnic or easy weeknight dinner. I used penne rigate for this recipe, but really any pasta will work: bow-ties, macaroni, etc.

The ranch and bacon are pretty much a guarantee that my family will devour this salad, and I love the color and texture that the carrots and peas add to it. Leftovers are amazing the next day!

16 oz (454 g) pasta, cooked and slightly cooled

16 oz (889 ml) sour cream

1 (1 oz [28 g]) package ranch dip mix

2 cups (250 g) diced rotisserie chicken

2 medium carrots, shredded

8 slices bacon, cooked and crumbled

1 ⅓ cups (178 g) frozen peas

Combine the cooked pasta, sour cream and ranch dip mix in a large bowl and stir until the pasta is evenly coated.

Stir in the remaining ingredients and refrigerate for at least 1 hour before serving.

NOTE: A delicious addition to this salad is cheese cubes. Cheddar is our favorite, but any cheese you have on hand would be great!

BBQ RANCH CHICKEN SALAD

YIELD: 4 SERVINGS

Fresh. Sweet. Different. Inspired by a salad at one of my favorite restaurants, this is one of my go-to light dinner recipes. It is absolutely packed with flavor, and the unique BBQ ranch dressing is a fun twist. This recipe is delicious with rotisserie chicken, but leftover grilled chicken is a good substitute.

I like to present this salad as a rainbow of colors on top of the lettuce. Everyone loves to see pretty food, and this salad is just that. Enjoy!

½ cup (118 ml) ranch dressing

¼ cup (59 ml) barbecue sauce

2 romaine hearts, chopped

2 Roma tomatoes, chopped

1 avocado, chopped

1 (15 ¼ oz [432 g]) can sweet corn, drained

1 (15 oz [425 g]) can black beans, rinsed and drained

2 cups (250 g) diced rotisserie chicken

1 English cucumber, seeded and chopped

2 oz (57 g) French fried onions

Combine the ranch dressing and barbecue sauce in a small bowl and set aside.

Add the lettuce to a large salad bowl and top with the remaining ingredients. Serve immediately with a drizzle of the BBQ ranch dressing.

CHAPTER 9

SLURPABLE SOUPS

Grab a spoon and get ready to dive into some amazing soup recipes! I can always count on my family to lick their bowls clean with any of these mouthwatering recipes. There's nothing more tantalizing than a bowl of steaming hot soup that is bursting with flavor, and that's what this chapter is all about.

Chicken and Buttermilk Dumplings (page 209), Coq au Vin (page 213) and Parmesan Chicken Corn Chowder (page 217) are just a few of the soups you'll find simmering in this chapter—make sure to check them out!

BROCCOLI CHEESE AND CHICKEN SOUP

YIELD: 6 TO 8 SERVINGS

I love soups that are hearty, and this one certainly fits the bill. Perfectly cheesy and packed with broccoli and chicken, each spoonful is creamy perfection. My boys are not all that into broccoli, but something magical happens when you add cheese to any vegetable; they love it!

1 tbsp (15 ml) olive oil

2 carrots, diced

½ onion, diced

1 stalk celery, diced

¼ cup (31 g) all-purpose flour

2 ½ cups (600 ml) low-sodium chicken broth

2 cups (459 g) broccoli florets

2 cups (250 g) shredded rotisserie chicken

2 cups (473 ml) milk

½ cup (80 g) diced roasted red peppers

8 oz (227 g) shredded cheddar cheese

12 oz (340 g) Velveeta, cut into 1" (2.5 cm) cubes

Heat the olive oil in a 4-quart (4-L) heavy-bottomed pot over medium-high heat. Add the carrots, onion and celery and sauté for about 4 to 5 minutes, or until the onion is soft and translucent.

Stir in the flour and cook for 1 minute, stirring frequently.

Whisk in the chicken broth and bring to a simmer over medium heat. Simmer for 5 minutes.

Add the broccoli and simmer for another 7 to 8 minutes, or until the broccoli is crisp-tender.

Stir in the shredded chicken, milk and roasted red peppers and cook for an additional 5 minutes.

Stir in the shredded cheddar cheese and Velveeta and cook, stirring almost continuously, for 5 minutes, or until the cheese has completely melted. Serve immediately.

NOTE: Cutting the Velveeta into cubes helps it to melt faster and more evenly. Don't skip this step!

CREAMY CHICKEN AND WILD RICE SOUP

YIELD: 6 SERVINGS

If my husband had his way, we'd have rice with every meal. His mom is from Peru, and that's what he grew up eating. I get extra bonus points when I put the rice in a warm, hearty soup like this one.

This soup is incredibly easy to prepare and tastes like it's been simmering on the stove all day. Perfect for a fall or winter evening.

¼ cup (57 g) unsalted butter, softened

2 stalks celery, diced

2 carrots, diced

½ onion, diced

1 shallot, diced

1 tsp poultry seasoning

1 tsp kosher salt

½ tsp fresh ground black pepper

¼ cup (31 g) all-purpose flour

1 cup (211 g) wild and whole grain brown rice blend

6 cups (1.4 L) low-sodium chicken broth + drippings from chicken

2 cups (480 ml) water

3 cups (375 g) diced rotisserie chicken

1 cup (237 ml) half-and-half

Melt the butter in a large stockpot over medium heat. Add the celery, carrots, onion and shallot and cook, stirring frequently, for 6 to 7 minutes. Stir in the poultry seasoning, salt and pepper and cook for 1 minute.

Sprinkle the flour over the vegetables and stir to evenly coat. Continue cooking, stirring frequently, for another 1 to 2 minutes.

Stir in the rice and gradually add the chicken broth, drippings and water. Bring to a boil, cover and reduce the heat to medium-low. Cook for 25 to 30 minutes, stirring occasionally, or until the rice is tender.

Add the chicken and cook for another 4 to 5 minutes, or until the chicken is heated through. Stir in the half-and-half and check for seasoning. Add more salt and pepper if necessary.

Ladle into bowls and serve.

NOTE: If you can't find a shallot, use the entire onion (instead of just half) and add two minced garlic cloves.

WHITE CHICKEN CHILI

YIELD: 6 SERVINGS

Chili is simple, comforting and delicious. I am a big fan of it—in fact, our whole family is! During football season, we make chili in our slow cooker almost every weekend. If you've never had white chili (made with chicken instead of beef), I think you'll find it to be just as hearty as the regular version, but way lighter in calories and fat. The flavors of the coriander and cumin go so nicely with the chicken and result in a very memorable dish.

We enjoy our white chili topped with sour cream, fresh cilantro and sliced jalapeños for an extra kick. If you want more of a creamy chili, stir in ½ cup (118 ml) of heavy cream or half-and-half right at the end. That's how my Aunt Rene makes hers, and it's fabulous!

2 tbsp (30 ml) vegetable oil

1 medium onion, diced

1 jalapeño, seeded and diced

2 cloves garlic, minced

1 tsp dried oregano

1 tsp ground coriander

1 tsp ground cumin

1 tsp kosher salt

½ tsp ground white pepper

3 cups (375 g) shredded rotisserie chicken

1 cup (240 ml) low-sodium chicken stock

1 (15 ½ oz [439 g]) can great northern beans, rinsed and drained

1 (4 oz [113 g]) can diced green chiles, do not drain

Heat the vegetable oil over medium-high heat in a large pot. Add the onion and jalapeño and sauté for 4 to 5 minutes, or until the onion is translucent. Add the minced garlic and sauté for 1 minute.

Stir in the oregano, coriander, cumin, salt, pepper and shredded chicken. You really want to coat the chicken in all those yummy spices.

Stir in the chicken stock, beans and green chiles and simmer for 20 minutes.

Serve with sour cream, cilantro and jalapeños if you'd like.

NOTE: Want to turn the heat up on this chili? Add another jalapeño to the mix!

BUFFALO CHICKEN SOUP

YIELD: 4 SERVINGS

I love this recipe because you can make this soup as hot or mild as you want to suit the needs of your family. Make sure you lean toward the more mild tastes because you can always add more buffalo sauce to individual bowls.

We like to serve this cheesy soup with carrots and celery for an authentic "buffalo" experience. If you can't find buffalo sauce, feel free to substitute in your favorite hot sauce.

3 tbsp (43 g) unsalted butter

1 carrot, diced

½ onion, diced

1 stalk celery, diced

1 clove garlic, minced

1 tsp salt

1 tsp fresh ground black pepper

⅓ cup (42 g) all-purpose flour

32 oz (907 ml) low-sodium chicken broth

½ cup (118 ml) whole milk

2 tbsp (30 ml) buffalo sauce

8 oz (227 g) shredded mozzarella cheese

5 oz (141 g) blue cheese crumbles

2 oz (57 g) grated Parmesan cheese

5 oz (142 g) shredded Monterey Jack cheese

2 cups (250 g) shredded rotisserie chicken

Melt the butter in a large heavy-bottomed pot over medium heat. Add the carrot, onion and celery and sauté for about 5 to 6 minutes, or until the onion is soft and translucent. Stir in the garlic and cook for about 1 minute. Season with salt and pepper.

Whisk in the flour and cook for 1 minute, stirring frequently.

Add the chicken broth and milk and bring to a simmer over medium heat. Simmer for 5 minutes.

Stir in the buffalo sauce and cheeses, reserving some of the blue cheese crumbles to use as toppings later, if you'd like. Stir continuously until the cheese is fully melted.

Add the chicken and cook for 5 minutes, or until the chicken is heated through.

Ladle into bowls and top with additional buffalo or hot sauce and blue cheese crumbles.

CHICKEN AND BUTTERMILK DUMPLINGS

YIELD: 6 SERVINGS

I felt obligated to include a chicken and dumplings recipe in this cookbook. Obligated and excited, that is. Every chicken cookbook should have some sort of chicken and dumplings recipe, and this one is going to blow you away with its home-cooked flavor and depth. And it all starts with a rotisserie chicken.

I used fresh veggies for this recipe because, I'll be honest, it makes a difference and it doesn't take much extra work at all. I made a version of my favorite biscuits for the dumplings and flavored them with fresh herbs. I used rosemary and parsley for this batch, but any fresh herbs will do the trick: parsley, thyme, oregano or dill—you really can't go wrong.

3 tbsp (43 g) unsalted butter

1 onion, diced

1 stalk celery, diced

2 carrots, diced

½ tsp salt

½ tsp fresh ground black pepper

¼ cup (31 g) all-purpose flour

3 cups (720 ml) low-sodium chicken broth

6 oz (170 g) green beans, cut into thirds

2 cups (250 g) diced rotisserie chicken

FOR THE DUMPLINGS

1 cup (125 g) all-purpose flour

1 tsp kosher salt

1 tsp baking powder

2 tbsp (5 g) chopped fresh herbs

2 tbsp (29 g) unsalted COLD butter, cubed

½ cup (118 ml) buttermilk

Melt the butter in a large pot over medium-high heat. Add the onion, celery and carrots and season with the salt and pepper. Cook for 5 to 6 minutes, or until the onion is soft and translucent. Add the flour and cook for 1 minute, stirring frequently.

Gradually add the chicken broth, stirring continuously. Bring the mixture to a boil and then reduce the heat to low and simmer for about 5 minutes.

While the mixture is simmering, we're going to get the dumplings going. Combine the flour, salt, baking powder and herbs in a medium bowl. Incorporate the butter into the dry ingredients until the mixture resembles coarse crumbs. Stir in the buttermilk just until combined. Don't overmix!

After the vegetable mixture has simmered for about 5 minutes, stir in the green beans and chicken.

Top with heaping spoonfuls of the dumpling dough. Cover and bring to a simmer, cooking for 11 to 13 minutes, or until the dumplings are cooked through. Sprinkle with some additional chopped herbs right before serving.

NOTE: If you saved the drippings from the rotisserie chicken, add those at the same time as the broth.

CHICKEN TORTILLA SOUP

YIELD: 6 SERVINGS

This soup is definitely one of my husband's favorite soups of all time. I'm game to make it any night of the week because it's so simple and delicious. We go a bit crazy with the toppings because that's the fun part. Tomatoes, onions, avocado, cheese and cilantro—I say YES to all of it!

1 tbsp (15 ml) olive oil

1 small onion, diced

2 cloves garlic, minced

2 tsp (5 g) chili powder

1 tsp cumin

½ tsp kosher salt

½ tsp fresh ground black pepper

2 cups (480 ml) reduced-sodium chicken broth

1 (28 oz [794 g]) can crushed tomatoes

1 (15 oz [425 g]) can black beans, rinsed and drained

1 (15 ¼ oz [432 g]) can corn, drained

1 (7 oz [198 g]) diced green chiles

2 ½ cups (315 g) shredded chicken

¼ cup (10 g) chopped fresh cilantro

Tortilla chips

TOPPING SUGGESTIONS

Sliced olives

Sliced green onions

Diced fresh tomatoes

Diced avocado

Shredded cheese

Cilantro

Heat the olive oil in a medium sauté pan over medium-high heat. Add the diced onion and sauté for 4 to 5 minutes, or until the onion is translucent. Stir in the minced garlic and continue sautéing for 1 minute. Add the chili powder, cumin, salt and pepper and cook for another 2 minutes.

Add the chicken broth and tomatoes and bring to a boil over medium heat. Simmer for 10 minutes.

Add the beans, corn, green chiles, chicken and cilantro. Simmer for an additional 10 minutes.

Ladle the soup into bowls and top with a handful of crushed tortilla chips and any toppings you want. Dig in!

COQ AU VIN

YIELD: 6 SERVINGS

I am fortunate enough to come from a family with French heritage. I grew up on great recipes like Coq Au Vin. There's nothing quite like it. Such a bold and flavorful stew such as this is hard to come by. It starts with bacon, butter and onion. You see where this is going, right?

Uncovering the pot after this hearty stew has simmered for a time releases such a delightfully heady aroma, it's hard not to ladle this goodness straight into your mouth. I have been known to take a few spoonfuls from the pot just to "test for seasoning," if you know what I mean. Serve this with some fresh, crusty French bread and prepare to be amazed. It's comfort food at its best.

½ pound (227 g) bacon, cut into ½ inch (13 mm) pieces

1 tbsp (14 g) butter

1 onion, diced

8 oz (227 g) sliced mushrooms

Salt and pepper, to taste

4 cloves garlic, minced

5 sprigs thyme

2 ½ cups (315 g) dark chicken pieces pulled off the rotisserie chicken

1 lb (454 g) small red potatoes, halved or quartered

1 (14 ½ oz [411 g]) can stewed tomatoes

1 cup (240 ml) low-sodium chicken stock

1 ½ cups (360 ml) dry red wine

Brown the bacon in a 4-quart (4-L) heavy-bottomed pot for about 8 to 10 minutes, or until the bacon gets nice and crispy. Remove with a slotted spoon to drain on a paper towel–lined plate.

Remove all but 1 tablespoon (15 ml) of the bacon grease and add 1 tablespoon (14 g) of butter to the pot. There's nothing better than bacon grease and butter together as a foundation for flavor.

Add the onion and mushrooms and cook, stirring frequently, until the onion is translucent and the mushrooms have released their moisture, about 5 to 6 minutes. Season with salt and pepper.

Stir in the garlic and thyme and continue cooking for 1 minute, stirring frequently. Add the chicken, potatoes, tomatoes, chicken stock and red wine. Bring to a simmer over medium-high heat, cover and continue cooking for 20 to 25 minutes, or until the potatoes are fork-tender.

Ladle the stew into bowls and garnish with fresh thyme sprigs and Parmesan cheese, if desired. It's very pretty that way.

HOME-STYLE CHICKEN NOODLE SOUP

YIELD: 8 SERVINGS

My Nana used to make us grandkids chicken noodle soup quite frequently during the winter months. I can't help but feel comforted every time I slurp down a spoonful of this goodness. It's ideal for chilly days or when you or a loved one is feeling under the weather. If you save the carcass of the rotisserie chicken, feel free to throw it in the pot for additional flavor and depth; just make sure all of the skin is removed first!

1 medium onion, diced

2 large carrots, diced

2 stalks celery, diced

3 tbsp (34 g) butter

Salt and pepper, to taste

1 bay leaf

1 tsp herbes de Provence

3 cups (375 g) diced rotisserie chicken, dark and white meat

64 oz (1.9 L) low-sodium chicken broth

8 oz (227 g) wide egg noodles

Sauté the onion, carrots and celery with the butter in a large pot over medium heat until the onion is translucent, about 5 to 6 minutes. Season with salt and pepper.

Stir in the bay leaf and herbes de Provence and cook for 1 minute. Add the chicken and broth and bring to a simmer. Cook for 10 minutes.

Add the egg noodles to the pot and simmer for 8 minutes, or until the noodles are tender.

Ladle into bowls and serve with crackers.

PARMESAN CHICKEN CORN CHOWDER

If you've never tried corn chowder before, you've missed out on a mouthwatering experience. This recipe takes corn chowder to a whole new level with the addition of Parmesan and chicken. It is incredibly hearty with the potatoes and chicken, and it's absolutely amazing when served in a bread bowl. Top with additional Parmesan cheese and sliced green onions for a pretty presentation that will have everyone reaching for their spoon.

2 tbsp (30 ml) olive oil

1 carrot, sliced

1 stalk celery, sliced

½ onion, diced

2 cups (480 ml) chicken broth

1 lb (454 g) red potatoes, washed and quartered or cubed, depending on size

¼ cup (57 g) butter

¼ cup (31 g) all-purpose flour

1 tsp salt

½ tsp fresh ground black pepper

2 cups (473 ml) whole milk

1 (14 ¾ oz [418 g]) can cream-style sweet corn

1 (12 oz [340 g]) package frozen corn

2 cups (250 g) shredded rotisserie chicken

6 oz (170 g) grated Parmesan cheese

Heat the olive oil in a large saucepan and sauté the carrot, celery and onion for 5 to 6 minutes, or until the onion is translucent.

Add the chicken broth and potatoes, cover and simmer for 12 to 15 minutes, or until the potatoes are tender.

Meanwhile, melt the butter in a small saucepan. Whisk in the flour, salt and pepper until nice and smooth. Gradually stir in the milk, whisking continuously until smooth. Bring the mixture to a boil over medium heat and continue cooking, whisking continuously, until the mixture has thickened. Remove from the heat.

Once the potatoes are tender, stir the flour and milk mixture into the simmering veggies. Stir in the corn, chicken and Parmesan cheese and cook for another 10 minutes, or until the cheese has melted and the chicken and corn are heated through.

My boys are suckers for fresh French and sourdough bread, so when I'm feeling generous, I serve this chowder in bread bowls or serve the bread alongside it. They lick their bowls clean no matter what.

ACKNOWLEDGMENTS

As I sit here writing this, I have tears of gratitude and joy in my eyes. It's a crazy thing, this whole "let's write a book!" business. There are days of jump-up-and-down excitement followed by days of doubt and anxiety, and every day is an adventure.

This book is only possible because of my fantastic readers at *Mom On Timeout*. Thank you for stopping by to find new recipes for your family and for getting a glimpse into mine. I appreciate every single comment, every pin and every share. It is because of you that I am able to stay home with my boys and cook in my pajamas and call it "work."

To the editors and designers at Page Street Publishing, thank you for your encouragement and support in making this book a true representation of me: my style, my photos, my recipes.

I want to thank each and every one of my blogging friends who patiently helped me along each step of the way. From narrowing down recipe ideas to choosing between two photos that would have looked identical to anyone else—you girls are just darn awesome! I so appreciate how generous you were with your expertise and experience.

Thank you to my sisters, Melissa and Ashley. You each helped in your own way, and that means so much to me. I appreciate all the reminders about family recipes that absolutely had to go in the book, your review of the recipes and your endless support and unwavering confidence in my ability to write this book even when the tasks seemed insurmountable. I love you guys!

To my brother Cliff, whose love of food and inspiration for recipe ideas kept me thinking and dreaming of new recipes that would make dinnertime easier and taste amazing. Also, a big thanks for keeping my dishwasher running through the endless loads of dishes that were created during recipe development. You are the BEST!!

To my dad. When I started to doubt myself, I thought of you. I thought of how proud you are of me, and just knowing that was enough to keep moving forward. Thank you for believing in me and supporting me through it all. I love you.

I want to thank my mom for raising me to believe that I can do anything, and for giving me the confidence and experience in the kitchen to have the desire and love of cooking and baking that I do. I miss you every single day.

I'd like to thank my sweet little boys, Reece and Bryce, for putting up with the endless hours on the computer and the ridiculous amount of chicken dinners we have eaten over the past year. You guys have been so patient, and your excitement for the book and your mommy being an "author" has made this whole thing so much more fun. You are my inspiration, each and every day, and I love you more than you could possibly know!

And last, but certainly not least, I'd like to thank my husband, Chris. For listening to me, comforting me, encouraging me and not letting me give up. Thank you for putting up with the endless amount of dishes and props all over the place and for providing me with your honest (brutally so!) feedback. It was priceless. Thank you for allowing me to spend the time to write this book, time taken away from our family, knowing that the end result would be worth it. I love you and appreciate all that you do for our family! Now, let's go get a steak!

ABOUT THE AUTHOR

Trish Rosenquist is the mom behind the popular blog *Mom On Timeout*. Her passion for creating and sharing family-friendly meals is what inspires her each and every day. Trish started her blog in 2011 as a creative outlet. She enjoys all aspects of blogging: photography, writing and most especially, cooking and baking!

Trish is the mother of two little boys, Reece and Bryce, and she is married to her college sweetheart, Chris. They live in Northern California and lead a busy life running around to soccer practice, swim meets, basketball games and so much more. They like to keep active and busy at all times.

Trish enjoys reading, gardening and spending time with her family.

Mom On Timeout has been featured on numerous popular sites including Today.com and MSN.com and in *Cosmopolitan*, *Woman's Day*, *Huffington Post*, *Self*, *Country Living*, *Relish*, *Good Housekeeping* and more!

You can find Trish online at MomOnTimeout.com, where she's busy developing and sharing new recipes for your family to enjoy.

INDEX